Contents

Contents

A-Z Guide of diseases and healing juices (cont...)

Raw Juices can save your life

Raw Juices Can Save Your Life

An A-Z guide
by Dr Sandra Cabot

With contributions from
Beverly Shamon-Turner and Audrey Tea

Raw Juices Can Save Your Life
An A - Z Guide - 2001
by **Dr Cabot, Sandra**

Disclaimer

The suggestions, ideas and treatments described in this book must not replace the care and direct supervision of a trained health care professional. All problems and concerns regarding your health require medical supervision. If you have any pre-existing medical disorders, you must consult your own doctor before following the suggestions in this book. If you are taking any prescribed medications you should check with your own doctor before using the recommendations in this book.

First published 2001 by WHAS
P. O. Box 54
COBBITTY NSW 2570 Australia
Ph: 02 4655 8542
www.whas.com.au
www.liverdoctor.com

SCB International Inc.
PO Box 5070
GLENDALE AZ 85312-5070 USA
Ph: 623 334 32 32
Copyright © 2001 Dr Sandra Cabot

First Edition printed November 2001 (Aust.)

ISBN 0958613710

Notice of rights

Printed by Griffin Press
Typeset by Concept Factory Pty Ltd
Courtesy of "*The Rainbow Warrior*"

Our Cartoons of "The Happy Vegetables and Fruits" and the "Lean Green Mama", were designed and illustrated by Karen Barboutis - Congratulations for a brilliant work of art!

A-Z Guide of diseases and healing juices (cont...)

Chapter Five

> ## *Dedication*
>
> This book is dedicated to my late maternal grandmother Susannah Dalton who migrated to Australia when she was 14 years of age in a ship called the Barrabool in 1924.
>
> ~

About the Author

Dr Sandra Cabot MBBS, DRCOG is a medical doctor who has extensive clinical experience in treating patients with weight problems, chronic medical problems, liver problems and hormonal imbalances. Dr Cabot works with other medical doctors and her team of naturopaths in Sydney Australia and Phoenix Arizona in the USA. Dr Sandra Cabot began studying nutritional medicine while she was a medical student and has been a pioneer in the area of holistic healing. She graduated in medicine with honours from the University of Adelaide, South Australia in 1975. During the early 1980s Dr Cabot worked as a volunteer in the largest missionary Christian hospital in Northern India, tending to the poor indigenous women.

In Australia she pilots herself to many cities and regional and country centres, where she is invited to conduct seminars and training workshops. Dr Cabot appears regularly on radio stations such as 2GB and 4BC where she is a health commentator. Her free magazine called "Ask Dr Sandra Cabot" is available through health food stores and many pharmacies. The newsletter can also be read on line at www.sandracabot.com

Contributors

About Beverly Shamon-Turner

Beverly Shamon-Turner, AdvDipNat, DipsMH, CMSc, Irid, Cl.Nutr, is a leading Australian Naturopath, Medical Herbalist, Clinical Nutritionist and Journalist. Her passion is natural medicine. She shares her knowledge with students as a lecturer at Naturopathic Colleges. Her many years of research and experience have given her the knowledge and ability to find and treat the causative factors of health problems.

About Audrey Tea

The indefatigable Audrey Tea has been cooking delicious and healthy meals for well over 50 years. Born and bred in Adelaide South Australia, where Audrey's culinary talents have tantalised the taste buds of thousands, she continues to design and test recipes in collaboration with Dr Sandra Cabot. While maintaining the principles of healthy metabolism, Audrey can prepare and cook dishes, which range from fabulous family meals, gourmet dinner party menus, quick snacks, special surprises and boutique sweet treats. This skill has taken her many years to perfect and yet despite this amazing talent, she remains incredibly humble and giving.

Audrey Tea is also a recipe tester and has had to make many modifications to conventional Western recipes that we once considered healthy. Audrey helps us to discover that healthy can be gourmet and indeed is usually much tastier and satisfying than the meals that were once considered traditional Australian cuisine. She has managed to make the recipes truly multicultural, which will introduce new flavours and health benefits to you by increasing diversification of your diet.

I have been fortunate to be a recipient of Audrey's meals over the years and I hope to continue to receive her regular gifts of treats. I am now delighted to be able to share these recipes with you and your family. They come with laughter and maternal healing vibrations, just like Audrey Tea herself. Audrey Tea accompanies Dr Sandra Cabot on many of her seminar tours and is always available to answer questions on healthy cooking and menu planning.

Introduction

Raw Juices can save Your Life

There is no doubt in my mind that raw juicing can save your life. I have seen it work miracles in some of my patients who were stuck on the merry-go-round of drug therapy. The juice from raw fruits and vegetables has powerful healing and rejuvenating properties that can help people with all sorts of health problems.

I have known about the healing power of raw juices from a very young age, because they were the only therapy that saved my grandmother's life. My grandmother, Susannah Dalton, was struck with a very severe form of a kidney disease called glomerulo-nephritis while she was still in her twenties. This was during the 1930's when very little was available to treat kidney disease. In glomerulo-nephritis, the immune system attacks the tubules of the kidneys causing widespread kidney inflammation and blood and protein in the urine. Susannah was truly at death's door when the hospital told my grandfather there was nothing further they could offer to save her life. Thankfully, my grandfather Harry, was a man ahead of his time and a hospital dietician. Harry took Susannah home and started a program of raw juicing. Harry gave her a glass of raw vegetable juice made alternatively from a vegetable growing above the ground and from a vegetable growing below the ground every hour. A miracle then started to occur, and over the next 6 weeks Susannah gradually regained her health. Her kidney inflammation settled down and her kidneys regained normal function. The concentrated vitamins, minerals and anti-oxidants in the juices had calmed down her immune system and put out the fire of inflammation. Susannah Dalton was a wonderful woman and lived to the ripe old age of 78 years. It must have been a labour of love for my grandfather, as in those days one did not have the luxury of easy to use juice-extracting machines.

Often in this technological age where computers diagnose diseases and perform surgery, we tend to minimise natural therapies. It seems incredulous that the simple act of drinking raw juices could turn around severe diseases, however I have seen it work in otherwise hopeless cases.

Juices are easily digested and absorbed and are superb for those with a poor appetite, nausea, digestive problems and an inflamed stomach or intestines. It is so much easier to drink a juice than chew your way through large amounts of fibrous raw vegetables, especially if you are feeling fatigued and disinterested in food.

Modern day medicine is focused on treating the symptoms of disease with suppressive drugs. Sometimes this is necessary when a disease is very aggressive and acute in onset, however raw juice therapy is something that should always be used, even in conjunction with drug use. I have seen many of my patients recover from chronic diseases after they started juicing, and this has been after they have tried many other things. People of all ages can benefit from juicing, especially the very young and old, or those with serious diseases such as cancer, immune dysfunction and liver problems.

Juices are a perfect medium in which to mix and dissolve nutritional powders, and will enhance their healing powers. The nutrients and herbs in powders are better absorbed than tablet forms of the same ingredients, and mixing them in juices enhances their solubility, digestion and absorption. The juices bring the healing nutrients to the cells in the surface of the mucous membrane of the gut in an easily absorbed form. This requires much less energy to assimilate than solid tablets, especially in people with inflamed mucous membranes in the intestines.

Juices can be combined in so many ways to make them palatable and even delicious. Their diverse colours and taste enable huge variety so that you will not get bored. For those who feel they need an extra boost there is nothing better than having a raw juice everyday. It will brighten up the day by providing extra energy and endurance.

Juices are easy on your intestines

Juices are packed with living enzymes to assist the digestive process, which means your gut, liver and pancreas do not have to work too hard to provide you with vital nutrients. This conserves vital body energy, which means that you do not feel heavy or weighed down after drinking juices. You can absorb up to 99% of their nutritional value. Juices supply a concentrated supply of vital nutrients. A medium size glass of carrot juice (250mls) is approximately equivalent to eating 500 grams (over one pound) of raw carrots. Eating so many carrots at one time would be hard on the jaws and teeth and would take a long time to get through.

Juices are unique because they allow the gut to receive very concentrated amounts of phyto-nutrients that could not be obtained by eating a normal amount of raw vegetables and fruits.

Ideally, you should consume a diet that consists of a high percentage of raw fruits and vegetables, with cooked vegetables and raw juices. If you find the juices too strong, simply dilute them with water or flavoured herbal teas according to your taste. If you are sensitive to fruit sugar (fructose), or are diabetic, then it is better to avoid fruit juices and use only vegetable juices.

Juices can reduce acidity and toxicity in the body

Many people consume a diet high in processed foods, along with tea, coffee and alcohol. This causes a build up of acids and metabolic waste products in the body, which can result in more inflammation. This acidic-state of the body can be neutralised by drinking raw juices. Celery, cucumber and cabbage juice are excellent to reduce acidity. This is an effective way to balance the pH levels (acid-base balance) in the body, which will dramatically increase energy and well being.

Raw juices are able to stimulate the function of the bowels, liver and kidneys, which increases the breakdown and elimination of toxic chemicals and waste products from the body. The raw juices can increase the quality and flow of the bile. This is very important in detoxification, because the liver pumps large amounts of toxic poisons out of the body through the bile. In some people, the biliary system is like a "sewer" in that it is laden with unhealthy fats and toxins. Little wonder that millions of people suffer with liver and gall bladder diseases and stones. If only they knew about the power of raw juicing and "The Liver Cleansing Diet", they would be able to keep their gall bladder, and enjoy a healthier life.

It is quite safe and very effective to go on a raw vegetable and fruit juice "fast" for 2 to 3 days. During these days you have nothing to eat except raw juice combinations, and raw vegetables and fruits. Diabetics cannot do this, as they must have regular protein and complex carbohydrates, but they can still enjoy raw juicing.

There are so many sick people on this planet searching for lasting solutions to their health problems. Furthermore, some of the drugs used to treat common ailments, can themselves cause diseases, and we call this drug-induced disease "iatrogenic disease". For example, non-steroidal anti-inflammatory drugs can damage the stomach, kidneys and the liver, if they are taken on a long-term basis. The cholesterol lowering drugs known as "statins" can cause severe muscle diseases. Some of the drugs used to lower blood sugar levels can cause liver disease.

A friend of mine who is a flying instructor was taking anti-inflammatory drugs for several months to reduce the pain of a back problem. After several weeks he found himself depressed and unable to remember the things he needed to be able to fly and instruct well. He was about to start anti-depressants, when I told him to stop the anti-inflammatory drugs and try "The Liver Cleansing Diet" and raw juicing. Within 2 weeks, his memory and mental abilities had returned and he could cope easily. He had been told he was suffering with stress!

Long-term antibiotics can cause severe liver damage, which can lead to immune dysfunction resulting in allergies and autoimmune diseases. Steroids like cortisone may lead to weight gain, high blood pressure, diabetes and osteoporosis. Also, these drugs become increasingly ineffective over long periods of time.

These problems led me to become a medical doctor who first likes to do no harm to her patients. This is why I have turned towards nutritional medicine and I have found it immensely satisfying.

The incidence of obesity and type 2 diabetes has tripled in the last 40 years because we are not in tune with our body's natural needs. It is true that "the food keeps getting faster and faster and we keep getting slower and slower"! You may be aware that in the early part of the year 2000, there was an emergency recall in the USA of a drug called "Rezeulin". Rezeulin had been initially released onto the market for diabetics to lower their blood sugar levels. Rezeulin caused severe liver damage in a significant percentage of diabetics, and some of these cases were fatal.

Introduction

We often tend to panic when we become sick and rush into taking drugs or having surgery. It is often better to sit down, relax and think for a while, so we can look at more natural alternatives. Can we change our diet and lifestyle, reduce stress, and take the time needed to truly heal ourselves? Yes, we can afford some more time for ourselves, and even if we need to take drugs, it is vitally important to start a program of raw juicing and raw foods. This is so important but rarely given the credibility it deserves.

Whilst I was lecturing in New Zealand, I met a very young woman with severe autoimmune liver disease. Her doctors did not know why she had developed this severe liver inflammation and had told her that she was going to need a liver transplant. During childhood, she had suffered with numerous colds and flues that had been treated with prolonged and excessive doses of antibiotics. These had probably been very significant in the genesis of her mysterious liver disease. If only her parents had not panicked and taken the time to consult a nutritional doctor and a specialist immunologist to check her immune system thoroughly. She could have controlled many of these infections with raw juices, dietary modification and nutritional supplements.

Another of my patients had come to see me suffering with longstanding obesity and had tried stomach stapling, many fad diets and tons of appetite suppressant drugs. These had damaged her liver and she had developed a "fatty liver", which made it impossible for her to lose weight. I convinced her to start juicing and to take a powerful liver tonic. She was quite desperate and agreed to try this program. After 12 months, she had reversed her fatty liver and had lost 37 kilograms in weight. In her case, it was vital to get her liver burning fat again. The juices had improved her liver function, changing her liver from a fat storing organ into a fat burning organ. She found that the juices quenched her appetite and gave her the energy to start exercising again.

Another patient came to see me complaining of weight excess, a facial rash and elevated liver enzymes. She had originally suffered with acne rosacea, which is a red pimply rash of the face. The doctor had given her long term tetracycline antibiotics for the acne, which had damaged her liver and made her face bright purple in colour. To overcome this drug induced side effect, she was taken off the tetracycline and given cortisone and antihistamines. The cortisone upset her heart causing severe palpitations and she then had to stop everything. She was very frustrated and had finally turned towards a natural solution for the imbalance in her body. I started her on a course of juices for her liver and immune system and within 3 months, all her problems had gone. Moreover, she had lost much of her excess weight.

It is surely time to turn back to the treasure house of nutritional healing, so that we can work on the causes of disease and rejuvenate the sick cells in our bodies back to health. I am always hearing stories from patients that make me saddened because they were not offered the benefit of using raw juices. Even though a program of raw juicing may to many, seem simple and nothing new, it is an incredibly powerful healing tool.

Sandra Cabot

Dr. Sandra Cabot

Chapter 1

Machines for Juicing

Everyone should have a juice-extractor machine in his or her kitchen. It is one of the best investments you will ever make for your health!

There are several types of juicers available, which vary in their abilities, quality and price.

Below we look at the various types of juicers.

Centrifugal Juicer

This type of juicer chops the produce into small pieces and then throws them against a spinning bowl that separates the fibre from the juice. They are not as efficient as the masticating types of juicers.

Advantages: Easy to clean
Relatively inexpensive

Disadvantages: Can be very noisy
Juicer may clog up if the produce is fed in too fast
Shorter life span
The juice is not completely extracted, so there is more waste

(The more expensive ones are better)

Grinder-Strainer/Masticator Juicer

Grinds the produce into very small particles, and presses or mashes them through a screen, which separates the juice from the fibre.

Advantages: Long life span (high quality machine parts)
Makes nut and seed spreads/butters
Makes dairy free "ice-cream" from frozen fruits
Easy to clean
Able to juice grasses, such as wheat grass
Middle price range
Can prepare fresh baby foods

Disadvantages: Heavy and cumbersome

Raw Juices can save your life

Hydraulic Press Juicers

This juicer uses a process of hydraulic press and grinder. The pressing action turns the fruits and vegetables into a paste, which is then pressed further, to extract the juice. It allows the maximum amount of juice to be separated from the fibre pulp.

Advantages: Long life span (high quality machine parts)
Able to juice grasses such as wheat grass

It is the most efficient juicer of all types, as it produces the maximum amount of juice from the fibre pulp.

Disadvantages: Is the most expensive type of juicer
Cannot make nut and seed spreads/butters

Dr. Sandra Cabot recommends the:

BREVILLE JUICE FOUNTAIN

For quick and easy juicing everyday.

Breville has recently released "The Juice Fountain" Featuring a powerful heavy duty motor system and a patented extra large feed chute, the Juice Fountain can juice whole fruit and vegetables in seconds.

There is no longer any need to cut apples into small pieces to make juice, The Juice Fountain is easy to use and even easier to clean.

With health organizations world wide encouraging people to eat more fruit and vegetables, the Juice Fountain couldn't have arrived at a better time!

The Breville Juice Fountain
is available from all leading department and electrical stores nationally. For further information on stockists please contact:
Breville Customer Service Support on 1300 139 798.

Dr Sandra Cabot also recommends the **"Samson" 6-IN-ONE, Multi-purpose "living" juice extractor.** The 'Samson's' gentle method of extracting liquid from fruit and vegetables creates a fresher tasting juice. The freshness of the 'Samson extracted juice' is attributed to the enzymes being kept alive. These enzymes are beneficial to the digestion and assimilation of nutrients, and also to the elimination of toxins in the body. The 'Samson' creates juice with up to 60% more nutrients compared to a centrifugal extractor. Only a living juicer will not damage enzymes. Enzymes die with heat, speed or friction.

- **10 year warranty on motor, 5 years on parts and labour**
- **Easy 1 minute cleaning**
- **Simple assembly**
- **Low speed ensures you get the highest nutrient value**
- **Higher yield with drier pulp**
- **Comes with 6 nozzles for creating different food**
- **3 squeezing strength positions**

❶ Fruit & vegetable juice extractor
❷ Wheatgrass, barley grass & herb juice extractor
❸ Frozen fruit dessert maker
❹ Meat, chicken & fish mincer
❺ Homogeniser for grains, nuts, seeds, seasoning & sauces
❻ Pasta maker

To Health By Choice
1800 021 069

The 'Samson' is the ultimate machine for juicing wheat grass and all leafy greens. By changing one attachment your Samson juice machine becomes a process for nut butters, frozen fruit desserts and mincer for meat, fish and chicken. It takes less than a minute to clean and comes with a 10-year warranty on the motor and a 30-day money back guarantee.

www.tohealth.com.au

Raw Juices can save your life

Chapter 2

General Guide to Juicing

What do raw fresh juices contain?

☆ Living enzymes to improve digestion and break down mucous. Enzymes are catalysts for the metabolic processes needed for digestion of food and the production of cellular energy.

☆ Living antibiotic substances to fight infections.

☆ Natural anti-inflammatory substances to reduce pain and the destruction of cells.

☆ Anti-oxidants such as vitamin C, vitamin E, flavonoids, beta carotene and other carotenoids, which fight cancer and inflammation.

☆ Phytochemicals which are substances in plants that can reduce many diseases. Categories of phyto-chemicals include - flavonoids, carotenoids, terpenes, coumarins, capsaicin, chlorophyll, indoles, isothiocyanates, lentinan and isoflavones. Inside one citrus fruit there are over 170 phyto-chemicals. Over 60 flavonoids found in citrus fruit, contain anti-inflammatory, and anti-tumour actions, reduce the tendency to form blood clots and have strong antioxidant activity. There are over 4000 different flavonoids known today, and food scientists believe there are many more yet to be discovered. Juicing is an effective and economical way to obtain these vital substances in their living form.

☆ Organic sulphur compounds to detoxify poisonous chemicals and drugs, and cleanse the liver and blood stream.

☆ Minerals such as magnesium, potassium, calcium, phosphorous, iron, copper, zinc, boron and selenium.

☆ Vitamin K is found in the dark green leafy vegetables and is beneficial for bone strength and the immune system. Vitamin K can also reduce heavy menstrual bleeding.

☆ Although some raw fruit juices contain significant amounts of simple sugars, such as fructose, because they are accompanied with a large variety of minerals and vitamins, the harmful effects of quickly absorbing refined sugars are not seen.

☆ Fluid from the juices prevents dehydration and aids kidney function.

How to buy and prepare fresh produce

☆ Try to choose produce that is fresh, unblemished and in season.

☆ Wash all the produce well and remove any bruised, blemished, or mouldy parts. Cut or slice the produce into pieces to fit into the input of your juice extractor. The white inner skin or pith (found just inside the tough outer skin) on citrus fruits, is replete with beneficial bioflavonoids, so try to conserve this, when preparing citrus fruits for juicing.

☆ The peel (if organic produce) and seeds of fruits such as grapes, watermelon, and rock melon, as well as citrus, can be juiced along with the fruit. The seeds from pawpaw are bitter in taste, and are best discarded. Fruit stones should be removed, as they will damage the juicer.

☆ Include the stems and leaves of the vegetables in the juice, as they are high in vitamins and minerals. If you suffer with kidney stones, do not include carrot tops, as they are high in oxalic acid, which can increase stone formation.

☆ Buy organic produce that is free of pesticides and insecticides where possible. If this is not possible, peel the produce to reduce consumption of toxic chemicals.

☆ Do not wash green leafy vegetables in hot water, nor leave them to soak in cold water for long periods of time, as this draws out the beneficial minerals.

☆ Frozen fruits and vegetables, or those that have been stored for long periods are not suitable for juicing.

☆ Ideally drink the juice within one hour of making it, otherwise it will be oxidised by the air and may develop a sour taste. However juices made in the morning can be stored for later the same day, or juices made at night can be stored for the next morning, provided you store them correctly. This must be in a jar with a tight lid, or in the refrigerator in a closed container, or in a jug with glad wrap over the top, to seal it tightly from the air.

☆ Some juices, such as very sweet fruit juices, or beet, dark green or bitter tasting juices may need diluting with pure water or herbal tea. You can also dilute strong flavours with celery, apple juice or cold flavoured herbal teas. Generally, juices for children should be diluted to improve the taste and increase the child's hydration. See our special section on juices and smoothies *on page 143* . Kids will love the taste while getting healthy at the same time.

☆ When making carrot juice, or indeed any juices, adding a small amount of citrus juice, will preserve the natural colour of the juice and reduce oxidation of its essential nutrients.

☆ Some people with irritable bowel syndrome, or a very sensitive stomach, may find that they cannot tolerate juices, which combine fruits and vegetables. In general, if you are like this, you will be safe by adding apple or pear to vegetable juices, but not other fruits. Celery seems to be well tolerated when it is mixed with fruit juices.

☆ If you are slimming, use mainly vegetable juices, as they contain less calories than fruit juices.

☆ You can use the fibre left behind after juicing to mix in pet food, or for compost.

☆ The juice machines are known as juice extractors and are suitable for vegetables and fruits.

☆ It is worthwhile getting a special citrus juicer for juicing citrus fruits, as it produces better results.

☆ You should feel free to experiment with different vegetable and fruit juice combinations, and you may come across a combination that really energises you. Make a note of particularly energising or tasty juice combinations in the My Favourite Recipes and Notes Section at the end of the book.

☆ Some people need to be careful with juicing as they have medical conditions that can be aggravated by a high consumption of simple sugars. These conditions are diabetes type 1 and type 2, hypoglycaemia and fungal infections. These people should avoid fruit juices, and are better to eat the whole fruit, as advised by their

Raw Juices can save your life

dietician. They can however gain tremendous benefits from raw vegetable juices, but must limit the intake of sweeter vegetable juices such as carrot or beetroot.

Can I pick my own leaves?

While walking through the park or the countryside, it is tempting to pick your own leaves to juice. Unfortunately there can be obstacles to the idealism of this behaviour.

Due to the prevalence of pollution from animals, industry, motor cars and insecticides, the plants can be spoiled and you could be getting more toxic chemicals than goodness. Other major problems can come from picking and ingesting a plant that looks like the 'real thing' but is its 'poisonous twin'. Most plants have a copy in nature that is poisonous or at least tastes bad. So, wisdom would suggest that in the case of any leafy greens such as dandelion, for instance, it might be best to cultivate a plant in a rockery or pot, where you can control its growth.

There are specialist nurseries, which cater to selling herbs, where you can buy a cultivated dandelion plant that you can grow, as you would any other herb. Two plants would give you all the leaves you need with minimal care. When the plant flowers, nip the bloom out before it dies and seeds, as this will stop the plant becoming a nuisance throughout the garden.

The juice from dandelion leaves is invaluable in the making of juice combinations, as it has a very high content of vitamins and minerals, which help in the treatment of many ailments. Dandelion is also an excellent liver tonic and blood purifier.

Quantities of juice

Most of our recipes should yield around (250 - 500mls)
$$= (8 - 16oz) = (1-2) \text{ cups of juice.}$$

However fruit and vegetables can vary significantly in their juice content because of seasonal weather conditions, attention to cultivation by the grower, and the freshness of the product. Be prepared to add a little more, or use less, to balance these factors.

Depending on how many of the family are drinking juices, prepare enough to allow up to 1/2 litre (3/4 pints) per person daily, starting with the first glass to be taken just before breakfast. Cover the remaining juice and keep refrigerated. To see really significant health benefits, you should aim for a minimum of 500mls (16 oz or 2 cups) per day, unless otherwise stated. This can include up to 50% water and/or herbal teas, used to dilute strong tasting juices.

Juice Combinations which are best avoided

There are some combinations of produce that do not mix well in juices. This can be because of the interaction of the individual plant's chemical constituents with those of another, resulting in a combination that does not sit well with the digestive system, or that tastes unpleasant.

If any combination of juices that you try does not make you feel good after drinking it, alter the balance of ingredients in the recipe to suit your particular taste, or dilute it with water or cold herbal teas.

The following juice combinations are best avoided -

⊗ Prune juice does not go well with cabbage, onion, watercress, or garlic.

⊗ Pear and tomato juice is not a good mix.

⊗ Grape juice with carrot juice can cause flatulence.

⊗ Garlic and onion juice does not taste good with fruit juice, except for tomato, lemon and orange.

⊗ Fig juice does not mix well with radish juice.

⊗ Blackberry juice does not mix well with beetroot or its leaves.

⊗ Apricot juice does not mix well with green vegetables or green leaves.

⊗ Cabbage, watercress, or turnip juice does not mix well with lemon, orange, or grapefruit.

Chapter 3

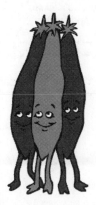

Table of the Healing Properties of Juices

Table of the Healing Properties of Juices

Type of plant	Available Nutrients & Phyto-chemicals	Healing Properties
Alfalfa Sprouts	*Vitamins*: B, C, E, K, folic acid & beta-carotene *Minerals*: magnesium, sulphur, chlorine, silicon, calcium, iron, zinc, sodium, potassium and phosphorous. High in phyto-estrogens.	An excellent source of chlorophyll and amino acids. Chlorophyll has a similar pattern of elements to that of haemoglobin, and so is very useful for building red blood cells. Helpful for anaemia. The chlorophyll also benefits the respiratory tract and lungs. Assists with weight loss. Supports liver function. Useful for menopausal symptoms, as it contains large amounts of phyto-estrogens.
Almond milk (made by blending whole almonds and water, and straining off water)	*Vitamins*: B & C *Minerals*: calcium, iron, phosphorous, potassium, magnesium and sulphur Amino acids	Supports the nervous system. Beneficial for muscle tone and body building. Excellent source of calcium for the teeth and bones.
Apple	*Vitamins*: B & C *Minerals*: potassium, calcium, phosphorous, iron, silicon and chlorine	High in the soluble fibre pectin, which soothes the intestines and reduces constipation. Improves colonic flora and reduces unfriendly colonic bacteria & parasites. Increases the elimination of toxins via the intestines.Improves digestion. Grated apple is excellent in cases of childhood diarrhoea. Reduces gallstones and gouty arthritis. Massages the gums and lowers cholesterol. Put the core, skin and flesh through the juicer to increase mineral and anti-oxidant content.
Apricot	*Vitamins*: B, C & beta-carotene *Minerals*: sodium, calcium, potassium, iron, magnesium and phosphorous	Excellent for skin problems. Acts as a blood tonic and helps to reduce anaemia. Helpful in cases of inflammatory bowel disease. Reduces acidity. Helpful for chronic cough and asthma.
Asparagus	*Vitamins*: B, C, folic acid and beta-carotene *Minerals*: calcium, iron, phosphorous, potassium and magnesium	Asparagus juice helps to break up oxalic acid crystals in the kidneys and muscular system. Thus it is good for the pain of rheumatism and arthritis. Reduces kidney stones.

Raw Juices can save your life

Table of the Healing Properties of Juices

Type of plant	Available Nutrients & Phyto-chemicals	Healing Properties
Avocado (this is best eaten, as it does not juice)	*Vitamins*: C, B and beta-carotene. *Minerals*: high in potassium, calcium, and iron and phosphorous. Contains beneficial oils for the cardiovascular system	Excellent nutritional food containing plentiful amounts of beneficial oil, vitamins and minerals. Helpful for peptic ulcers and inflammation of digestive system.
Banana (great in smoothies)	*Vitamins*: B & C *Minerals*: calcium, sodium, magnesium and potassium	Excellent for children and adults with a poor appetite and digestive problems. Excellent for stomach and intestinal inflammation such as colitis and Crohn's disease. Ripe bananas reduce diarrhoea. High sugar content makes it a high-energy food. Not beneficial when unripe and green.
Bean Sprouts (such as sprouted mung beans, alfalfa, wheat berry, chickpeas, lentils and aduki beans etc)	*Vitamins*: B, C, E and beta-carotene *Minerals*: calcium, iron, phosphorous and potassium.	Sprouted seeds, pulses and grains provide high amounts of easily digested protein. The Chinese use sprouts to cleanse and detoxify the body.
Beans, string	*Vitamins*: B, C, beta-carotene & folic acid *Minerals*: Calcium, Iron, Potassium	According to Oriental medicine, beans are thought to strengthen the kidneys and liver. They are an excellent source of protein. Because of the slow release of their glucose content, they are an excellent food for diabetics. They help to keep blood sugar levels stable.
Beetroot and tops (can use the tops as well if desired)	*Vitamins*: C, B, folic acid & beta-carotene *Minerals*: chlorine, manganese, calcium, iron, sodium, phosphorous, potassium, chromium, and magnesium	Good cleanser for the liver, biliary system and gall bladder. Beneficial in cases of iron deficiency anaemia. Improves energy and vitality. Reduces hardening and blockage of the arteries (atherosclerosis).
Berries *See Blackberries Blueberries Raspberries Strawberries*	*Vitamins*: C & beta-carotene *Minerals*: potassium, calcium and iron.	Excellent general tonic and skin cleanser. Mild laxative and diuretic. Improves kidney function.

Type of plant	Available Nutrients & Phyto-chemicals	Healing Properties
Blackberries	*Vitamins*: B, C & beta-carotene *Minerals*: calcium, iron andpotassium	General tonic and blood and skin cleanser. Helpful for catarrh and intestinal inflammation. Helpful for anaemia, arthritis and fluid retention. Unripe berries are helpful for menstrual cramps and haemorrhages. Blackberry leaf tea helps to relieve a sore throat.
Blueberries	*Vitamins*: B, C & beta-carotene *Minerals*: calcium and potassium	Good blood cleanser and antiseptic. Useful in cases of anaemia, diarrhoea, intestinal inflammation and skin problems.
Broccoli	*Vitamins*: high levels of B, C, folic acid & beta-carotene. *Minerals*: calcium, iron, phosphorous, potassium and sulphur	Excellent for weight loss. Helpful for high blood pressure, liver problems and constipation.
Brussels Sprouts	*Vitamins*: B, C, folic acid and beta-carotene *Minerals*: phosphorous, calcium, iron, potassium and sulphur	Reduce insulin problems, which is useful in those with Syndrome X. Good general tonic and helpful for constipation, liver problems and obesity.
Cabbage	*Vitamins*: C, B, folic acid and beta-carotene *Minerals*: very high in sulphur and chlorine. Also contains calcium, potassium and iodine	Excellent for many digestive and intestinal problems, such as bowel infections, parasites, bowel ulceration, and colitis. Excellent liver tonic. Reduces gallstones and disorders of the bile ducts. Good skin cleanser in cases of acne and skin infections
Cantaloupe (rockmelon)	*Vitamins*: B, C and beta-carotene. *Minerals*: calcium and potassium	Useful in feverish states, high blood pressure, constipation, arthritis, intestinal gas/bloating, and kidney/bladder problems
Capsicum (see Peppers)		
Carob	*Vitamins*: B and beta-carotene *Minerals*: calcium, iron, phosphorous, copper and magnesium	Carob powder can be used as a chocolate substitute. It has less fat & calories than chocolate, but has no oxalic acid or caffeine, as does chocolate. Carob is a good source of protein and carbohydrate and has excellent general health benefits. Carob powder is good in cases of 'non-specific diarrhoea'.

Raw Juices can save your life

Table of the Healing Properties of Juices

Type of plant	Available Nutrients & Phyto-chemicals	Healing Properties
Carrot	*Vitamins*: B, C, D, E, K and beta-carotene *Minerals*: calcium, iron, phosphorous, chromium, magnesium, potassium, sodium, iodine, silica, chlorine and sulphur	Improves night vision and promotes healthy eyes. Excellent for skin problems. Reduces inflammation of the mucous membranes in the intestines & respiratory tract. Is a liver cleanser and tonic. Healing effect in ulcerous and inflamed conditions of the stomach and intestines. Superb for increasing vitality and vigour. It contains an insulin-like compound and thus small amounts can be used in juice mixtures for diabetics and those with Syndrome X. Promotes high quality breast milk and a healthy pregnancy. Excellent for growing children.
Cauliflower	*Vitamins*: B, C, folic acid & beta-carotene *Minerals*: calcium, iron, phosphorous, sulphur and potassium	Excellent blood purifier and liver tonic. Useful for kidney/bladder disorders and constipation.
Celery	*Vitamins*: B and C *Minerals*: calcium, iron, phosphorous, potassium, magnesium, sodium, iron and sulphur	Reduces acidity, which is beneficial in cases of arthritis, gout and toxicity. Excellent in cases of stomach acidity and reflux. Natural diuretic, which reduces fluid retention.Calms the nervous system. Helps to balance the blood's PH levels (acid-base balance). Excellent for weight reduction as it lessens a 'sweet-tooth'. Helpful for insomnia, kidney/bladder problems and constipation Cut pieces into short lengths (2.5cm = 1 inch) so that no long fibres become twisted in the juicer.
Cherries	*Vitamins*: B, C & beta-carotene *Minerals*: phosphorous, potassium & iron Darker cherries contain greater amounts of magnesium, iron & silicon	Good blood cleanser. Valuable for anaemia, rheumatism, asthma, high blood pressure, constipation and cramps. Cherries have a low Glycaemic Index (GI) and are therefore a good fruit for those with Syndrome X or diabetes.

Chillies
(see Peppers)

Type of plant	Available Nutrients & Phyto-chemicals	Healing Properties
Citrus fruits *See* Orange Grapefruit	*Vitamins*: Very high in C. The white pith contains large amounts of valuable bioflavonoids *Minerals*: potassium, magnesium, sodium, calcium, phosphorous	Soothes inflamed mucous membranes. Reduces the severity of the common cold and flues. Natural antibiotic, anti-inflammatory and cleansing properties. Strengthens the immune system and reduces the risk of cancer. Powerful anti-oxidant with anti-ageing properties. Improves collagen formation and skin tone.
Coconut	*Vitamins*: B, C and E *Minerals*: calcium, phosphorous, potassium and iron	Coconut milk helps to relieve sore throats and peptic ulcers. The flesh contains natural cholesterol, which can be used by the body to manufacture hormones and cell membranes. Good source of protein. Coconut milk/cream is an excellent base for non-dairy "smoothies" containing other fruits and/or flaxseed oil. Pleasing to the palate of people of all ages.
Coriander	*Vitamins*: B, C & folic acid *Minerals*: potassium, sodium, and magnesium. The active ingredient in Coriander is 1 per cent of volatile oil. It contains about 5 per cent of ash as well as malic acid, tannin and some fatty matter.	The essential oil in coriander stimulates the flow of bile & digestive juices. It relieves gas, and reduces stomach and intestinal cramps. Fresh coriander has been used successfully for appetite loss and indigestion. Traditional herbalists valued coriander for counteracting stomach-upsets caused by laxative herbs, and to reduce asthma. Coriander has also been used to treat coughs & bladder complaints. It is an aromatic herb with a delicious and distinctive taste. Excellent for salads and juices.
Cranberry	*Vitamins*: C, B and beta-carotene *Minerals*: sodium, potassium, copper, calcium, manganese, phosphorous, iron, zinc, magnesium and sulphur	Cranberry has antiseptic properties and contains benzoic and quinic acids, which reduce urinary tract infections. Is an excellent cleanser and skin tonic. Do not add sugar to cranberry as the berries then become acid-forming

Raw Juices can save your life

Table of the Healing Properties of Juices

Type of plant	Available Nutrients & Phyto-chemicals	Healing Properties
Cucumber	*Vitamins:* B, C and beta-carotene. *Minerals:* sodium, silica, manganese, sulphur, potassium, calcium, phosphorous, chlorine and magnesium	Excellent diuretic properties to reduce fluid retention. Anti-inflammatory effect on the urinary tract, the gums and skin. Rich content of silica is beneficial for the hair, nails and skin. Reduces hair loss. Its enzyme content aids protein digestion. High potassium levels are helpful for high blood pressure. Reduces acidity in cases of arthritis and rheumatic conditions. Reduces kidney stones.
Dandelion	*Vitamins:* High levels of beta-carotene, folic acid, B and good levels of C. *Minerals:* sodium and high in potassium, calcium, iron and magnesium.	Cleanses the liver & biliary system. Stimulates the flow of bile and is useful in all liver complaints. General tonic aiding anaemic and malnourished states. Is also a blood builder. Helpful in eczema and constipation. Excellent for arthritic and rheumatic conditions, as it normalises the acid balance of the body. Juice is extracted from the leaves of the plant, which should be fresh.
Dates	*Vitamins:* Beta-carotene, B and E. *Minerals:* calcium, iron, sulphur and very high potassium levels	Natural carbohydrate food, easily digested, valuable in cases of low blood pressure, nervous states and anaemia. Excellent for nursing mothers.
Fennel	*Vitamins:* B, C and beta-carotene *Minerals:* calcium, chromium, cobalt, iron, magnesium, manganese, phosphorous, potassium, selenium, silicon, sodium and zinc	Has a calming effect on digestion, stimulates gastric secretions and reduces intestinal cramps. Reduces intestinal gas, flatulence and bloating.
Figs	*Vitamins:* B, E, C and beta-carotene. *Minerals:* calcium, iron, phosphorous, magnesium and potassium	Figs are alkaline-forming and so are beneficial in gout and rheumatism. They are helpful for constipation and emaciation (inability to gain weight). Helpful for cases of low blood pressure. They have the highest sugar content [about 50%] of common fruits, and so may be best avoided by those with blood sugar or candida problems.

Type of plant	Available Nutrients & Phyto-chemicals	Healing Properties
Garlic cloves (This also applies to all vegetables in the "Allium Family" such as leeks, onions, shallots, spring onions and chives)	*Vitamins*: B and C *Minerals*: selenium, phosphorous, iron, chromium, calcium magnesium and potassium. Contains organic sulphur	Contains allicin, which fights infection and reduces LDL cholesterol. Promotes a healthy cardiovascular system. Is a good liver and bile cleanser. Natural antibiotic for the whole body. Dispels intestinal parasites. Helps the immune system to fight cancer.
Ginger root	*Vitamins*: C *Minerals*: copper, potassium, sodium, iron, calcium, zinc, phosphorous and magnesium	Natural antibiotic for the whole body. Reduces congestion and mucous production. Fights the common cold and flu. Natural remedy against nausea and travel sickness. Inhibits the formation of inflammatory prostaglandins, thereby reducing the pain of arthritis. Inhibits the formation of blood clots and lowers LDL cholesterol.
Grapes	*Vitamins*: B, C and beta-carotene *Minerals*: phosphorous: iron, calcium and potassium Pectin	Provide a quick boost of energy. Have laxative and diuretic properties. Helps in anaemia and blood disorders. Reduces the inflammation of arthritis. Supports skin, kidney and liver function. Helps eliminate acid from the body. Improves the complexion. When juicing pass the whole fruit with skins intact, through the juicing machine. Keep in the refrigerator.
Grapefruit	*Vitamins*: B, E, beta-carotene, biotin, and inositol. Very high levels of vitamin C *Minerals*: calcium, iron, phosphorous and potassium	Aids in the removal and dissolving of excess calcium in the joints. Helpful for catarrh, gallstones, obesity, sluggish liver function, digestive problems and respiratory and skin problems.
Guava	*Vitamins*: B, C and beta-carotene *Minerals*: calcium, iron, potassium and phosphorous	Helpful for digestive problems and diarrhoea. Improves circulation and reduces catarrh and asthma.
Honeydew melon	*Vitamins*: B, C and beta-carotene *Minerals*: calcium, phosphorous, potassium and iron	Excellent diuretic properties. Useful for kidney and bladder problems. Reduces rheumatic and skin conditions. Aids in weight loss.

Raw Juices can save your life

Table of the Healing Properties of Juices

Type of plant	Available Nutrients & Phyto-chemicals	Healing Properties
Horseradish	*Vitamins:* B and C. *Minerals:* phosphorous, calcium, sulphur and high in potassium	Dissolves mucous. Natural antibiotic and very helpful for colds, sinusitis, tonsillitis, bronchitis and asthma. Stimulates the appetite and the flow of bile. Can be used in salads or juices in small amounts only. Excess amounts can be irritating to the stomach.
Kelp (kombu) and other sea vegetables such as arame, wakame, nori, hijiki, dulse etc.	*Vitamins:* B and beta-carotene. *Minerals:* calcium, magnesium, potassium, iron, phosphorous, iodine, selenium and zinc	An excellent source of minerals and trace elements not readily obtainable in the commonly eaten vegetables of Western diets. The rich mineral content of sea vegetables benefits the nervous system and strengthens the immune system. Their high mineral content boosts the metabolism and thyroid function, so that sea vegetables are an excellent aid to weight loss. Helpful in maintaining strong bones. Alginic acid, which is present in much seaweed, binds with heavy metals such as lead, mercury and cadmium and increases their elimination from the body.
Lemons	*Vitamins:* C and P (from its citrine content). *Minerals:* potassium, magnesium and small amounts of calcium	Reduce the tendency to haemorrhage, blood clots and high blood pressure. Lemon juice is a powerful solvent in cases of arthritis and gout, thus reducing acid deposits in the joints. Excellent cleanser for the liver, bowel and blood stream. Relieve sore throats, coughs, colds, catarrh and asthma. Reduce nasal mucous production. Avoid in cases of peptic ulcers. Can use in salad dressings.
Lettuce	*Vitamins:* B, C and folic acid *Minerals:* calcium, silica, potassium, phosphorous, sulphur, iodine, iron and magnesium	Has cooling and diuretic properties. Reduces acidity and so is helpful for arthritis and cystitis. Contains a natural sedative called lactucarium as well as magnesium, which help to calm the nervous system and improve sleep.

Type of plant	Available Nutrients & Phyto-chemicals	Healing Properties
Mango	*Vitamins*: B and C, and high in beta-carotene *Minerals*: calcium, iron, phosphorous and magnesium	Helpful for inflammation of the gut and mucous membranes. Reduces respiratory tract inflammation. Improves digestion. Enhances skin appearance and healing.
Nectarines	*Vitamins*: C and beta-carotene *Minerals*: calcium, iron and phosphorous	Support digestive activity. Useful in bronchitis, asthma, rheumatic states and high blood pressure. Can reduce cystitis.
Parsley	*Vitamins*: B, folic acid and high in C *Minerals*: sodium, calcium, potassium, phosphorous, copper, manganese. High in iron and chlorophyll.	Excellent cleanser of the liver, kidneys and blood stream. Reduces gallstones and kidney stones. Helpful for arthritis and urinary tract infections. Excellent diuretic. Maintains healthy blood vessels and eyes.
Pawpaw [Papaya]	*Vitamins*: B, high in C and beta - carotene *Minerals*: phosphorous, potassium, iron and calcium	Contains the digestive enzyme called papain, a valuable aid for digestion. Cleanses and tones the stomach and intestines. Useful in cases of intestinal ulceration. Reduces the tendency to blood clotting.
Peaches	*Vitamins*: B, C and beta-carotene *Minerals*: potassium, sodium, magnesium, calcium, phosphorous and iron	Quick energy booster. Improves the complexion. Reduces stomach and kidney inflammation. Helpful for bronchitis and constipation. Useful in anaemia and high blood pressure. Assists in the removal of intestinal worms.
Pears	*Vitamins*: B and C *Minerals*: calcium, iron, phosphorous, potassium, sodium and magnesium	Reduces acidity. Useful in those with digestive problems, irritable bowel, constipation and colitis. Excellent for those intolerant to salicylates or suffering with food allergies.
Peppers - Sweet Green, red, orange, yellow & purple (members of capsicum family)The green peppers are harder to digest as they are less ripe. Roasting or char-grilling peppers will enhance their sweetness.	*Vitamins*: beta-carotene, folic acid, B and high in C *Minerals*: potassium, silica, iron, calcium, phosphorous, magnesium	Powerful cleanser of the intestines and liver. High antioxidant content aids the circulation and improves vision.

Raw Juices can save your life

Type of plant	Available Nutrients & Phyto-chemicals	Healing Properties
Peppers - Chilli There are more than 200 types of chilli. Red chillies are not always hotter than green chillies, but they are probably riper. They range in taste from mild to blisteringly hot	*Vitamins:* beta-carotene, folic acid, vitamin E and very high in vitamin C. *Minerals:* potassium, magnesium, sodium, and selenium.	The hotness of chillies comes from capsaicin, which is found in the seeds, white membranes and the flesh. Capsaicin can block the activation of cancer-causing chemicals. Chillies stimulate the brain to release endorphin chemicals, which improve the mood. Chillies are powerful decongestants and can relieve sinus and catarrh. They improve circulation and increase the metabolic rate thus assisting weight loss. In excess amounts they can irritate the intestinal lining and stomach. Caution must be used in those with digestive/intestinal problems.
Pineapple	*Vitamins:* B, E and C. *Minerals:* calcium, sodium, phosphorous, potassium, chlorine and magnesium.	Has an anti-inflammatory property, which is of use in arthritis. Supports digestion of proteins (it contains digestive enzymes such as bromelain). Mild laxative & diuretic properties. Reduces mucous congestion. Helpful in bronchitis, asthma, sinusitis and wherever excess catarrh is a problem. Assists in weight reduction.
Pomegranates	*Vitamins:* B and C. *Minerals:* sodium, potassium and magnesium	Helps to eradicate intestinal parasites such as worms, giardia, candida and amoeba etc. Good blood and kidney cleanser. Mild laxative.
Potatoes - sweet	*Vitamins:* B, C, and very high levels of beta-carotene *Minerals:* calcium, iron, phosphorous, potassium, silicon, chlorine and sodium	Excellent for building body strength. Easily digestable and soothing for stomach ulcers and inflammation of the colon. Eases diarrhoea and haemorrhoids.
Potatoes - regular There are thousands of varieties. Discard potatoes with green patches as these contain toxins called solanines.	*Vitamins:* B and C. *Minerals:* iron, potassium, phosphorous	Good source of energy as they are high in protein, complex carbohydrates and fibre. Soothing to the stomach and intestines.

Type of plant	Available Nutrients & Phyto-chemicals	Healing Properties
Prunes	*Vitamins*: B, C and beta-carotene *Minerals*: calcium, iron, phosphorous and potassium	Beneficial in anaemia and low blood pressure. Reduce constipation and flatulence. Those who suffer from haemorrhoids benefit from taking fresh or dried prunes and their juice. Excellent for sore throats.
Radish & its leaves There are several types - round ruby red, longer white tipped, Chinese radishes etc.	*Vitamins*: B, C, folic acid and beta-carotene *Minerals*: calcium, iron, phosphorous, silica, sodium, potassium, magnesium, iodine and chlorine	Excellent liver and bile cleanser. Reduces gall-stones and kidney stones. Excellent diuretic. Is a natural antibiotic for the whole body. Clears mucous from the respiratory tract and reduces sinus and hay fever. Excellent for goitre. Beneficial for the hair, nails and teeth.
Raisins	*Vitamins*: B and beta-carotene *Minerals*: calcium, phosphorous, iron and potassium	Builds strength. Useful in constipation, anaemia and fatigue.
Raspberries - Black	*Vitamins*: B and C *Minerals*: iron, potassium and phosphorous	Reduces intestinal parasites. Relieves menstrual cramps.
Raspberries - Red	Red also have beta-carotene	Reduces constipation and high blood pressure. Assists with weight loss. Raspberry leaves are excellent for diarrhoea.
Rhubarb	*Vitamins*: B and C and beta-carotene *Minerals*: calcium, iron, phosphorous, potassium and sodium	Rhubarb improves the flow of saliva, bile and gastric juices. It helps to support the muscular action of the bowels and small intestines. Reduces intestinal parasites and constipation. Its health benefits are most apparent when eaten raw and in very small quantities (as in a mixed juice). Rhubarb contains high levels of oxalic acid and sufferers of arthritis and kidney stones should avoid it. The leaves must not be eaten, as they can be toxic.

Table of the Healing Properties of Juices

Type of plant	Available Nutrients & Phyto-chemicals	Healing Properties
Spinach	*Vitamins*: B, C, K, Choline, Inositol, folic acid and beta-carotene *Minerals*: iron, iodine, calcium, phosphorous, potassium and sulphur	Heals the lining of the digestive tract. Improves vision. Reduces arthritic pain. Choline and inositol maintain healthy blood vessels. Supports kidney and liver function. Excellent in cases of anaemia. Reduces heavy menstrual bleeding. Reduces fatigue and constipation.
Strawberries	*Vitamins*: B, C & beta-carotene *Minerals*: potassium, calcium, iron and phosphorous	Excellent skin cleanser. Mild laxative & diuretic effect. Helpful for high blood pressure, gout, and rheumatism.
Tomatoes	*Vitamins*: B, C & K. Carotenes including Lycopene, which has anti-cancer properties. *Minerals*: potassium, calcium, iron, phosphorous and iodine	Good liver and bile cleanser. Antiseptic properties to reduce infections. Helpful in high blood pressure. Helpful for gout and kidney/bladder problems. Contains nicotinic acid, which helps to reduce cholesterol. Organic or vine-ripened tomatoes are preferable.
Turnip **Turnip Root**	*Vitamins*: B, C, E & beta-carotene *Minerals*: calcium, iron, phosphorous and potassium	Good liver and bile cleanser, as it has a slightly bitter taste. Best combined with carrot or apple juice. Good in cases of under active thyroid gland or thyroid gland cysts (multi-nodular goitre).
Turnip Leaves	*Vitamins*: B, C, E, K, folic acid & beta-carotene *Minerals*: iron, phosphorous, and very high levels of calcium.	Helpful in cases of anaemia, poor appetite and digestive problems. Reduces high blood pressure, gout and bladder ailments. Excellent for diabetics. Good blood cleanser. The leaves contain easily absorbed calcium - thus excellent for osteoporosis. Strengthens bones, nails, teeth and hair.
Watercress	*Vitamins*: B, E, C, folic acid & beta-carotene *Minerals*: very high in sulphur. Also contains calcium, iron, sodium, magnesium, phosphorous, chlorine, potassium and iodine	Excellent cleanser for the liver, bile ducts & gall bladder. Supports kidney function and reduces fluid retention. Skin cleanser. Useful in arthritis and gout. Best mixed with other juices.

Type of plant	Available Nutrients & Phyto-chemicals	Healing Properties
Watermelon	*Vitamins*: B, C and beta-carotene. *Minerals*: calcium, iron and very high in potassium.	Supports kidney and bladder function. The seeds dilate capillaries thus reducing blood pressure. Is a cooling food - reduces hot flushes & refreshes the thirst. Helpful in depression.
Wheat grass	*Vitamins*: B, C, E, K, folic acid, B17 and beta-carotene *Minerals*: calcium, zinc potassium, phosphorous, sodium, sulphur & cobalt. Very high in chlorophyll.	Powerful cleanser and detoxifier of the blood and liver. Strengthens the immune system. Reduces high blood pressure and increases energy levels. Anti-ageing capabilities.

Important Notes:

☆ The juice recipes can be varied according to your taste.

☆ If you are sensitive/allergic to any of the ingredients, you may eliminate them.

☆ If you find that you do not enjoy the taste, replace with a fruit or vegetable that you enjoy.

If any of the ingredients such as horseradish, garlic, onion, ginger or radish etc. cause digestive/abdominal discomfort, there are several things that you can do---

☆ Reduce the quantities, as even **a very small amount** will help

☆ Have the juice **just before** you eat your meal

☆ Dilute the juice with water, or herbal teas, or flavoured herbal teas (available in supermarkets)

Yellowing of the skin

Many of the fruits and vegetables used for juicing contain plentiful amounts of the beneficial phyto-chemical called beta-carotene. Beta-carotene is a powerful antioxidant, which reduces the risk of many types of cancer. Once levels of beta-carotene build up in the body, a slight yellowing or bronzing of the skin may occur. This is more apparent on the pale areas of the body such as the inner arms and palms. This is nothing to worry about, as it has nothing to do with vitamin A toxicity. Beta-carotene will not be converted into vitamin A unless the body needs more vitamin A. High levels of beta-carotene in the body will not lead to vitamin A toxicity, and indeed will reduce your chances of cancer. The bronzing of the skin gives a healthy glowing appearance to the complexion.

Chapter 4

A - Z Guide
of Diseases
& Healing Juices

Acne

Acne can result in permanent facial scars, poor self-image and psychological distress, causing untold anguish for the sufferer. When the free flow of oils through the skin becomes blocked, the skin becomes irritated and inflamed. The eating of refined sugars, full-cream dairy products and deep-fried foods will worsen acne.

The large surges in sex hormones during adolescence, particularly testosterone, can cause severe flare-ups of acne.

Mature onset acne may be due to hormonal imbalances, especially a deficiency of oestrogen.

Women with Polycystic Ovarian Syndrome produce excessive amounts of male hormones, which may result in acne.

Acne Rosacea is more common in mature persons and results in a red pimply rash around the cheeks, nose and chin. Acne Rosacea is due to a combination of hormonal imbalances and liver dysfunction.

The skin, being the largest organ of elimination in the body, will act as an 'overflow' to help clean excess waste out of the body. Acne can be greatly reduced by a change in diet and cleansing of the blood stream.

Juice Recipe for Acne

1	medium carrot
1	stick celery
1	medium beetroot with leaves
½	cup watercress leaves
2	dandelion leaves
¼ cm	(thin slice) of fresh ginger root
1	clove of fresh garlic (optional)
1	slice (about 3cms) fresh pineapple

Wash all ingredients, trim, remove any blemishes, and cut into pieces to fit juicer. Leave skins on where possible to retain important enzymes.

Options:
If dandelion leaves are not available, use parsley or spinach.

Raw Juices can save your life

- Carrot is high in beta-carotene, which assists skin repair.
- Beetroot, celery and dandelion have a cleansing action.
- Dandelion improves liver function, which is vital in all skin disorders. Its zinc content is important for hormone balance and skin healing.

Useful supplements:

Selenium, zinc and vitamin E reduce acne and scarring.

Olive leaf extract is a natural antibiotic to reduce skin infections.

Hormonal factors may also need to be addressed, particularly in women, as there are hormonal treatments that can reduce the effect of excessive male hormones (androgens) on the skin. These consist of some types of oral contraceptives and anti-male hormones such as Androcur. Such hormonal treatments can completely control acne if prescribed correctly. **For more advice call the Hormone Advisory Service on 02 4655 8855.**

Allergies

Allergies can manifest as a variety of problems such as -
- Asthma and coughing attacks
- Sinus and hay fever
- Red itchy swollen eyes, which may discharge watery fluids and mucous
- Skin rashes
- General itching of the body or throat
- Hives
- Severe life threatening reactions known as "anaphylactic reactions", requiring urgent medical attention.

Causes of allergies
Hereditary factors are important and there is often a family history of allergies.
Long term overexposure to drugs, especially antibiotics.
Adverse drug reactions.
Hypersensitivity to airborne pollens and pollution.
Hypersensitivity to food additives or contaminants such as pesticides, colourings, flavourings and preservatives.

Infections with fungal or bacterial organisms may sensitise the immune system and lead to leaky gut. These things may bring on allergies.

Immune dysfunction associated with auto-immune diseases.

Liver dysfunction, which results in an increased work load for the immune system.

Anti-Allergy Juice number one

1	radish
1	clove garlic or ½ red onion
1	carrot
1	pear
2	cabbage leaves

Anti-Allergy Juice number two

¼	medium pineapple
1	red chilli (optional)
1	red or green capsicum
1	pear

Anti-Allergy Juice number three

1 cm	fresh ginger root
1	apple
1	carrot
2	dandelion leaves or 2 cabbage leaves
½	red onion

Wash all ingredients, trim, remove any blemishes, and cut into pieces to fit juicer.

If you find these juices too pungent or strong, you may dilute them with water or cold herbal flavoured teas.

Anti-Allergy "Smoothie" Drink

1 cup	rice milk, almond milk or coconut milk
1	ripe banana
1	pear
1 tbsp	cold pressed flaxseed oil
1 tbsp	freshly ground flaxseed (use food processor or coffee grinder)
Pinch	ground nutmeg

Place all ingredients in a blender and blend until smooth. Sprinkle with nutmeg

Useful supplements and foods

Organic produce is highly desirable in those with allergies, as it is free of pesticides and additives that can aggravate allergies.

Selenium and zinc reduce inflammation

Essential fatty acids found in flaxseed oil, olive oil and oily fish

Garlic and horseradish tablets

Vitamin C and bioflavonoids

Organic sulphur such as MSM powder

Avoid long term use of Echinacea in allergic conditions

Liver friendly foods such as artichoke, cruciferous vegetables (cauliflower, cabbage, broccoli & Brussels sprouts) and eggs (provided you are not allergic to them)

Anaemia

The main function of red blood cells is to transport oxygen from the lungs to the body tissues and exchange it for carbon dioxide. The iron-containing protein inside the red blood cells, which transports the oxygen, is called haemoglobin. If you have a tendency to fatigue, this could point to a deficiency in haemoglobin. You may feel breathless when you exert yourself, because of a lack of oxygen and a build up of carbon dioxide in the body cells. Serious cases of anaemia bring on states of utter exhaustion.

Increased iron requirements occur in pregnant and breast-feeding women, infants during growth spurts, and elderly persons with digestive problems, menstruating women and teenage girls.

Menstruating women are particularly susceptible to anaemia because of the monthly blood loss they incur. Anaemia may also result from other sources of blood loss, or as a result of malabsorption of iron. Anaemia can be the result of deficient red blood cell production in the bone marrow from poor diet, certain medications or chronic diseases. Anaemia may also result from diseases and infections that destroy red blood cells such as malaria, adverse reactions to some drugs and haemolytic anaemia, which can occur in auto-immune diseases. Red blood cells that are abnormally shaped (such as in spherocytosis), or red blood cells that contain abnormal haemoglobin (such as thalassaemia), are susceptible to damage, which can result in anaemia.

Strict vegetarians (vegans) are at a higher risk of anaemia from deficiencies of iron and/or vitamin B 12.

Green leafy vegetables, as in the recipe below, are of benefit to anyone suffering from any type of anaemia. This is because the chlorophyll molecule in green vegetables is very similar to the haemoglobin molecule. These green vegetables are also high in iron and vitamin K.

Blood Building Juice

1	sprig parsley
1	small beetroot with some stem and leaves
1	medium carrot
3	small spinach/silverbeet leaves
½	cup wheatgrass - available in Supermarket in fruit & vegetable section
2	dandelion leaves or 2 turnip leaves
½	cup blackberries or raspberries
1 tsp	kelp powder

Wash, trim and chop and pass through juicer. Dilute if desired.

Raw Juices can save your life

Useful supplements:

A good multi-vitamin and mineral supplement should be taken containing iron, vitamin C, folic acid, vitamin B 12, copper and vitamin E. Essential fatty acid supplements containing a combination of flaxseed, evening primrose oil and lecithin will help the red blood cell membranes.

ANGINA *See Heart Conditions page 99*

ANTIBIOTICS - NATURAL

Many people suffer with chronic or recurrent infections, or take repeated courses of antibiotic drugs, which can impair the function of the liver and the immune system. Hidden infections are a common source of poor health and immune dysfunction. We call these hidden infections "sub-clinical infections". They may not be recognised because they only produce vague generalised symptoms such as fatigue, headaches, aches and pains and possibly intermittent fevers and sweating. The source of the infection may remain elusive and hidden. These sub-clinical infections with viruses, bacteria or parasites may be harboured secretly in the teeth, gums, sinuses, ears, lungs, bones, lymph glands or the intestines. Sometimes they can be in the liver or tucked away behind abdominal organs.

Antibiotic drugs may not work efficiently because the infection may continue to survive without oxygen (anaerobic infection), the organisms may be resistant to the drugs, or the blood supply to the infected tissue may not be good enough to carry therapeutic doses of the antibiotics to where they are needed. People continue to eat unhealthy foods and smoke cigarettes, all of which can produce pus and feed the infection.

Some people put up with these hidden infections for many years and accept that poor health is just the norm for them. These infections occur in unhealthy tissues and continue to release bacteria or other pathogenic micro-organisms into the blood stream. These bacteria can seed other organs where they flourish, causing such things as abscesses and heart disease. It is not particularly effective to rely upon long-term courses of antibiotic drugs, as the infecting organisms often become resistant to their action, and the antibiotics may cause serious organ damage.

Chapter 4

To control these hidden health-destroying infections, we must revitalise the dead and infected tissue and fight the micro-organisms with natural antibiotics. Thankfully, these infections do not become resistant to the powerful action of these natural antibiotics.

People can benefit from this natural antibiotic juice combination if they suffer with ---

    Chronic or recurrent bronchitis or asthma
    Bronchiectasis
    Cystic Fibrosis Disease
    Recurrent colds and flues
    Recurrent ear and sinus infections
    Recurrent cystitis or vaginitis
    Candida
    Unfriendly micro-organisms in the gut (dysbiosis)
    Helicobacter Pylori infection of the stomach
    Chronic fatigue syndrome or post- viral syndrome
    Malaria in its recurrent form
    Fatigue after infection with malaria, ticks or intestinal parasites
    Recurrent skin infections and boils
    Chronic ulcers
    Infected cysts
    Fungal infections of the toes and nails
    Dandruff of the scalp
    Acne
    Hepatitis A, B or C
    Chronic gum and tooth infections
    Periodontal disease of the gums
    Recurrent herpes
    Glandular fever (Epstein Barr Virus)
    Sarcoidosis
    Tuberculosis
    Aids or HIV

And indeed any chronic or recurrent infections

Antibiotic Juice Recipe

This juice combination acts as a powerful antibiotic and antiseptic, and when taken regularly can fight infections directly. One glass (at least 300-400mls) must be taken every day, and in many people twice daily.

1	carrot
1	beetroot including some green tops
2	spinach leaves
1 to 2	apples - skin on
½ cm	fresh ginger root
½ cm	horseradish root
1 to ½	clove garlic (optional) or ½ red onion
½ cup	watercress (optional)

Wash all ingredients, trim, chop, and put through juicer. Dilute with water or cold herbal tea to begin with, or if too pungent.

Options:

If you prefer this juice to be sweeter, add more apples, or 1 pear (skin on), or 2 slices of watermelon.

If you are uncertain of your tolerance to strong juices, start off by diluting 1 part juice to 1 part water, and gradually work up to full juice strength if possible. Even if you find that you can only tolerate this juice in diluted form, it will still have a powerful antibiotic effect.

Even though the garlic is highly effective, if you cannot tolerate garlic, leave it out.

> Horseradish is one of the most valuable concentrated foods. It is excellent to dissolve excess mucous, particularly in the respiratory system.
> Onion is a natural antibiotic and can reduce catarrh and infected mucus.
> Garlic contains allicin, which fights infection and is a natural antibiotic for the whole body
> Apple helps restore balance to the intestinal flora and reduces unfriendly colonic bacteria

Watercress has high levels of sulphur, which acts as a natural antibiotic and cleanser.

Carrot has high levels of beta-carotene to strengthen the mucous membranes against attack.

Natural antibiotic supplements should be taken, which will strengthen the immune system and reduce the growth of disease-causing (pathogenic) micro-organisms. The most effective are -

Olive leaf extract capsules 2000 to 3000mg daily with food (1000mg with each meal). In children an elixir (liquid) form of olive leaf extract can be used instead of capsules. A specialist paediatrician should assess children with recurrent infections.

A complete selenium formula containing selenium, zinc and vitamin C available in tablet form - 2 to 4 tablets daily.

MSM plus vitamin C powder - 1 flat teaspoon daily in juice. MSM is organic sulphur in a highly bio-available form.

ARTHRITIS

A life with arthritis is one of pain and immobility, which severely restricts one's lifestyle.

The causes of arthritis include -

Incorrect diet with an excess of processed foods, alcohol and meat, and a lack of raw vegetables and fruits.

Dehydration due to excess consumption of tea, coffee and sweet soda drinks, and a deficiency of water.

Trauma to joints from sports injuries or accidents.

Excess weight, which leads to premature wear and tear on the joints.

Lack of exercise and reduced fitness.

Auto-immune diseases such as Lupus, rheumatoid etc.

Celery Balancer

This juice will reduce acidity and inflammation in the joints. It is helpful for all types of arthritis and especially gouty arthritis.

4	stems of celery
1	medium carrot
2	medium apples, core out, skin on
200g	alfalfa sprouts - must be fresh
Small	handful of grapes
½ to 1	clove garlic (optional)
1	sprig parsley

Wash all ingredients, trim, chop, and put through juicer.
If the juice causes flatulence, remove the grapes from the recipe.

> Allicin, a substance in garlic, helps to wash away the sand-like waste in the joints.
> Parsley supports kidney function and reduces acidity.
> Grapes have an alkaline effect and help to reduce uric acid levels.

Pain-eze Juice

1cm	fresh ginger root
¼	pineapple
1	apple, core out, skin on
½	Lebanese cucumber or similar amount of any green cucumber
¼	grapefruit*

* May not be suitable if citrus aggravates your particular condition, or if you suffer from a salicylate sensitivity

Remove dry rough pieces of skin from pineapple but retain as much as you can. Wash, trim and chop all ingredients and put through juicer.

> Grapefruit contains organic salicylic acid and is one of the most valuable fruits for dissolving inorganic calcium, which may have settled in the cartilage of the joints.
> Pineapple is of great benefit in arthritic conditions and its bromelain content helps to dissolve waste material that may have accumulated in the joints

Cucumber reduces acidity in arthritic/rheumatic conditions.
Ginger has components, which inhibit the formation of inflammatory prostaglandins and thus reduce the pain of arthritis.

Useful supplements for arthritis and/or osteoporosis -

A Bone and Joint Nutrients capsule containing a combination of -
Calcium hydroxyapatite
Magnesium
Manganese
Zinc
Copper
Silica
Horsetail
Selenium
Vitamin D
Glucosamine

ASTHMA

Asthma is produced by -
Constriction (or spasm) of the bronchial tubes
An excessive amount of mucous production in the bronchial tubes.

These abnormalities narrow the airways, so that the amount of air entering the lungs decreases.

Asthma is caused by an over-reaction of the bronchial tubes to the following -
Airborne pollutants, smoke and pollens
Viral infections of the respiratory tract
Food allergies
Stress
Sudden changes in the environmental temperature
Exercise
Immune dysfunction, which is often triggered by poor diet

Symptoms of asthma
Shortness of breath and rapid breathing
Coughing and wheezing
Anxiety and restlessness

Asthma can be very dangerous, as the lung function can deteriorate quickly without producing the characteristic wheezing sounds. Thus it is important that asthmatics measure their lung function at home regularly with a simple machine called a "peak expiratory flow meter". This meter can be obtained at pharmacies. You should be instructed by your doctor in how to use this meter. This practise is especially important in children, in whom asthma attacks can be fatal.

Juice for asthmatics

1	carrot
1	orange or ½ grapefruit
½ cm	fresh ginger root
1	clove garlic or ½ red onion
2	cabbage leaves
10 cm	slice pineapple

If you want it sweeter, you can add 1 apple or 1 pear
Wash, trim and chop all ingredients and pass through the juicer

The above juice will reduce inflammation in the lungs, reduce mucous production and help to strengthen the immune system.

The antibiotic juice *(see page 47)* is also of great benefit to asthmatics who suffer with frequent respiratory infections.

Useful foods and supplements -
Magnesium tablets
Selenium and zinc
Vitamin C and bioflavonoids
MSM powder - ½ tsp once or twice daily, in the juice can be of benefit
Essential fatty acids - cold pressed flaxseed oil, salmon oil, cod liver oil

The diet should contain plenty of raw fruits and vegetables and oily fish. Those with excess mucous in the lungs and a productive cough should avoid all dairy products and margarine.

BLOOD CLOTS - *see Varicose Veins page 138*

BLOOD PRESSURE

The condition of high blood pressure is known as hypertension.

High blood pressure is a common problem and is associated with an increased risk of heart attacks and strokes. It is very important to take high blood pressure seriously and it must be well controlled and regularly supervised. Blood pressure most commonly occurs during middle age and is more common in the overweight.

Causes of high blood pressure

Most cases of high blood pressure are caused by hardening and/or blockage of the arteries. These diseased blood vessels become narrowed and inflexible, and thus the heart must exert more pressure to pump the blood through the blood vessels. Hardened blood vessels are less elastic and do not dilate properly which increases the pressure inside them.

Kidney disease can cause high blood pressure.

Stress and anxiety, which can cause an imbalance in the autonomic nervous system via excess production of adrenalin.

Symptoms of high blood pressure -

There are often no symptoms at all, and the raised blood pressure is found during a routine checkup. Possible symptoms are -

Headaches

Foggy brain syndrome - leading to poor memory, inability to concentrate, mental slowness etc.

Fatigue

Insomnia

Deteriorating vision

Shortness of breath

Raw Juices can save your life

Juice for high blood pressure

2	sticks celery
½	cucumber
½ cup	chopped parsley
½ cup	chopped fennel
1	spring onion or 1 clove garlic
1	apple
1	orange or ½ grapefruit

Wash, trim and chop all ingredients and pass through the juicer. Drink 2 glasses daily.

This juice will improve kidney function and reduce hardening and blockage of the arteries.

"Smoothie" for high blood pressure

1	banana
2cm	slice pineapple, skin removed
1 cup	oat milk, rice milk, almond milk or coconut milk
1 tbsp	ground flaxseed

Place all ingredients in a blender and blend until smooth.

Useful supplements -
Magnesium tablets - 2 tablets twice daily
Vitamin C and bioflavonoids
Cold pressed flaxseed oil
The herbs ginkgo biloba and bilberry

BODY SHAPING - *See also "Cellulite - page 64" & "Weight Excess - page 139"*

It is generally accepted that there are 4 different body shapes - Lymphatic, Gynaeoid, Android, and Thyroid.

Each Body Type has unique hormonal and metabolic characteristics, which explains why some people put on weight easily and others don't. It also explains which area of your body will tend to accumulate the excess body fat. The "Body Shaping Diet Book" gives an eating plan for each of the 4 different Body Types. This eating plan enables you to lose weight from where you need to lose the weight, as it balances the hormones and metabolism for your Body Type.

There are two major body organs that contribute to controlling the metabolic rate. These are the Liver and the Thyroid gland and if these organs are healthy, you will lose weight much more efficiently.

The following juices have been designed to help balance the metabolism for each of the 4 different Body Types.

Lymphatic Body Type

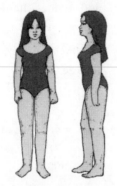 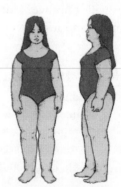

Lymphatic Ideal   **Lymphatic Overweight**

In those with a Lymphatic Body Type, weight gain occurs over the entire body. Their lymphatic system is dysfunctional leading to fluid retention, which makes them look fatter than they really are. Lymphatic types have a very sluggish metabolism or low metabolic rate, which causes them to gain weight very easily. They may not enjoy exercise and often crave dairy products such as milk, cheese, cream and ice cream, which may overload their lymphatic system and slow down metabolism.

It is important for Lymphatic Body Types to avoid dairy products and drink plenty of water every day. Regular exercise should be encouraged.

The following juice reduces fluid retention, improves the lymphatic system and boosts metabolism.

L- Body Type Juice

1cm	slice fresh ginger root
2	sticks celery
½	grapefruit
½	Lebanese cucumber
½	red radish
5cm	slice fresh pineapple

Ginger and other spicy foods such as chilli, curry, coriander, tumeric and mustard etc. will increase the metabolic rate.

Celery, pineapple and cucumber have diuretic properties and reduce fluid retention.

Grapefruit is known to promote weight loss

Radish contains iodine and stimulates the thyroid gland thereby increasing metabolism

L - Body Type Figure Control nutrients are:

Fenugreek, Rutin, Selenium, Celery, Horseradish, Fennel, Kelp, Cayenne and Vitamin B6.

Gynaeoid Body Type

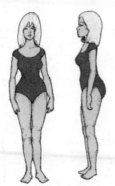
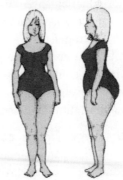

Gynaeoid Ideal   **Gynaeoid Overweight**

Gynaeoid type women gain weight around the hips and thighs leading to a pear shape. They have curvy feminine figures and their hormone balance leans predominantly to the oestrogenic side. This is called "oestrogen dominance", which increases fat deposits around the hips, thighs, and buttocks. This is often associated with cellulite.

Their food cravings often involve both fats and refined sugars, which consumed together, increase the body's sensitivity to oestrogen.

Gynaeoid shaped women benefit from reducing their consumption of foods combining unhealthy fats and sugars. They should also increase high-fibre fruit and vegetables, as dietary fibre reduces oestrogen dominance.

G-Body Type Juice

½	cup alfalfa sprouts
1to 2	dandelion leaves
1	broccoli floret
1	spinach leaf
1	small carrot
¼	cantaloupe (rockmelon)
1	small piece turnip root

Alfalfa sprouts and spinach support thyroid function and promote weight loss

Dandelion cleanses the liver, helps weight control and contains zinc for hormonal balance

Broccoli contains organic sulphur, which helps the liver to metabolise excess oestrogens

Carrots have insulin-like properties, which balance blood sugar

Turnip root contains substances, which speed up the metabolism and encourage weight loss

Cantaloupe stimulates the metabolism

G - Body Type figure control nutrients are:

The herbs - wild yam, parsley piert, vitex agnus castus and gymnema sylvestre and the mineral chromium picolinate.

Android Body Type

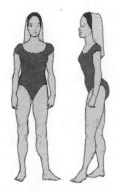 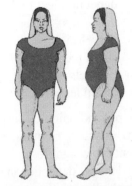

Android Ideal **Android Overweight**

Android body types have broad shoulders and narrow hips. They do not have a narrow waist and are not curvy like the Gynaeoid types. They have a broad rib cage and strong muscular arms and legs. They are physically strong and often make good athletes. Fat deposition occurs in the upper body, on the trunk and abdomen, which may produce an "apple shape". Android Body Types tend to produce excess amounts of male hormones (androgens), which may aggravate their weight problems.

Food cravings include rich, cholesterol/salty foods and carbohydrates. Apple shaped persons with excess weight in the abdominal area, are prone to the chemical imbalance of Syndrome X. This means that they have problems with insulin metabolism, which makes them store fat, especially in the abdominal area. For more information on how to overcome Syndrome X, see my new book titled "Cant Lose Weight? You could have Syndrome X - the chemical imbalance that makes you store fat."

A - Body Type Juice

1	red apple
1	dandelion leaf or 1 broccoli floret
1	vine - ripened tomato
½	grapefruit
2	slices red onion
2	Brussels sprout
2	turnip leaves

Raw apple and onion cleanse the liver and reduce cholesterol

Tomato contains nicotinic acid, which reduces cholesterol and is excellent for weight loss

Turnip leaves, dandelion and Brussels sprouts contain sulphur to cleanse the liver and improve the flow of bile.

A - Body Type figure control nutrients are -

The herbs St Mary's Thistle, red clover, hops, Dong Quai, the fibre called chitosan, and the liver nutrients choline and inositol.

Thyroid Body Type

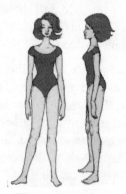
Thyroid Ideal

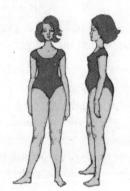
Thyroid Overweight

The fine-boned body of the ballet dancer or fashion model is typical of the 'Thyroid' type figure. Weight gain does not occur easily because thyroid types have a very high metabolic rate.

Thyroid Body Types tend to over use stimulants, such as nicotine, caffeine, sugar and artificial sweeteners. This may lead to adrenal gland exhaustion or "burn out".

Cravings for sugary foods, such as a donut with coffee and a cigarette for breakfast are common choices for Thyroid types.

Dietary changes should include regular meals containing complex carbohydrates such as wholegrain breads and legumes and protein from hormone-free chicken, lean red meats, eggs and seafood. Regular exercise is needed to help build bone density.

T- Body Type Juice

1	beetroot
1	spinach leaf
1	carrot
4	green string beans
1	small bunch grapes

Wash and chop produce and pass all through the juicer

Spinach is helpful for the circulation, aiding low blood pressure, which is often present in thyroid body types. It boosts energy levels.
Carrot is high in calcium and improves vitality and vigour.
String beans contain calcium for the bones and reduce sugar cravings.
Grapes are an excellent source of energy.

T - Body Type figure control nutrients are-

Liquorice, ginseng, glutamine, vitamin B 5, zinc, magnesium and chromium picolinate.

For more information on nutrients for Your Body Type, Phone a Body Shaping counsellor on 02 4655 8855

To discover your Body Type NOW visit www.weightcontroldoctor.com and do the interactive questionnaire on line.

Chapter 4

BREAST LUMPS AND TENDERNESS

Breast tenderness and breast lumps are common and worrying problems. All women with breast symptoms are worried that it may signal cancer, which is not surprising as breast cancer affects 1 in 11 Australian women, and every day in Australia, around 6 women die from breast cancer.

The causes of breast tenderness and/or lumps are -

Hormonal imbalance during the menstrual cycle
Poor diet lacking in antioxidants
Side effects of the oral contraceptive pill or hormone replacement therapy
Poorly fitting bras

Juice for breast symptoms

1	orange or 1 mandarin
1	grapefruit
2	sticks celery
2	dandelion or cabbage leaves
1	spring onion or 1 clove garlic
1	medium carrot

3 to 4 drops of Phytolacca tincture can be added to the juice and is available in health food stores. Phytolacca is a herb that cleanses the lymphatic system.

The diet should be high in raw fruits and vegetables and dairy products should be completely avoided.

Useful supplements -

Selenium 100mcg daily
Vitamin B complex or Brewer's yeast
Vitamin E
Cold pressed Flaxseed oil and evening primrose oil
Natural progesterone cream or lozenges can help to reduce oestrogen dominance, and may reduce hormonal cases of breast tenderness.

Raw Juices can save your life

BRONCHITIS

The term bronchitis indicates inflammation of the bronchial tubes leading to the lungs.

Causes are -

Viral and bacterial infections
Exposure to pollution and cigarette smoke.
Allergies such as asthma.
Mechanical problems such as bronchiectasis.

Bronchitis Juice

2	slices fresh pineapple
1	orange
½	lemon or ½ grapefruit
1	clove garlic (optional, but it is very effective)
2 slices	red onion
½ cm	fresh ginger root
2cm slice	horseradish
¼ cup	hot water
1 tspn	honey

Steep onion in hot water for 10 minutes. Drain water into a glass. Add honey. Discard onion.
Trim rough bits off pineapple skin but leave as much green as possible. Wash other ingredients, trim, chop and then pass through juicer. Add juice to onion water.

Drink or sip 1 cup, 2 or 3 times daily.

You may dilute this juice (1 part juice to 1 part water) and gradually increase its strength, as your gut becomes more tolerant.

Onion and garlic contain substances, which help to loosen and drain mucous
Honey soothes the mucous membranes
Orange and lemon juices are high in Vitamin C, which is a natural antibiotic.
Pineapple and horseradish break down unhealthy mucous.

Chapter 4

Useful foods & supplements

Vitamin C and MSM powder can help to boost the immune system.

Olive leaf capsules and elixir can help to fight respiratory tract infections. Avoid mucous producing foods such as dairy products, margarine and processed foods.

CANCER

Patients with cancer need to use strategies to strengthen their immune system so that it is better able to fight the spread of cancerous tissue. Many patients with cancer, especially in the advanced stages, are unable to ingest large meals and suffer with nausea and poor appetite. Cancer patients will often have difficulty in obtaining adequate nutrition from cooked meals and/or large amounts of raw fruits and vegetables. Raw juicing is of paramount importance to cancer patients, as it can provide concentrated amounts of antioxidants and phyto-nutrients to strengthen the immune system. Without raw juicing it is usually impossible to provide enough nutrients to support the immune system.

Juice for cancer patients

2	spinach leaves or 2 dandelion leaves
1	apple
½	papaya
1	carrot
1	clove garlic or 1 spring onion
½	Beetroot
2	Shiitake mushrooms (remove stems & wipe caps clean)
3	drops Echinacea tincture (if available from health food store)

Wash, chop and pass through juicer. To vary this juice from time to time, you can substitute with the following ingredients:

Mango, broccoli, Brussels sprouts, cabbage leaves, cauliflower, kale, bokchoy, red onion, pear, and indeed any deeply/brightly coloured vegetables.

"Smoothie" for Immune Strength

1	cup oat, almond, coconut or soymilk
1	banana or ½ large mango
1	tbsp whey protein powder
2	drops vanilla essence (optional)
1	tbsp freshly ground flaxseed
¼	tsp nutmeg powder to sprinkle on the top of the smoothie

Place all ingredients in a blender and blend until smooth. Serve with 3 fresh organic strawberries or ½ cup black or red berries on the side.

Useful supplements

Vitamin C

Selenium and zinc

Echinacea

Lactoferrin - also found in whey protein concentrate

CANDIDA

Candida albicans is a yeast-like organism that can produce inflammation in the various mucous membranes of the body - such as those found in the vagina, intestines, anus, and mouth, and the skin. It only becomes an opportunistic infection when the host's immune system is compromised.

Causes of Candida

Side effects of drugs such as antibiotics and steroids

Hormonal imbalances during pregnancy or from the contraceptive pill

A diet high in sugar and refined carbohydrates

Diabetes

AIDS caused by the virus known as HIV

A weakened immune system

Juice for Candida

2	cabbage leaves
1	clove garlic or ½ red onion
4	green string beans
1	carrot
1	orange or ½ grapefruit

Wash, trim and chop and pass all through the juicer and drink daily

Useful supplements

Acidophilus
Olive leaf extract capsules or elixir
Garlic and horseradish capsules
Selenium and zinc

CELLULITE

Just beneath the skin is the tissue referred to as the subcutaneous layer. It binds the skin to the bones or connective tissues beneath its surface. The subcutaneous layer is thinner in women than in men, and as women age it becomes much thinner. The fat cells, which lie below and within the subcutaneous layer, become larger because of the thinning of connective tissues. These fat cells can now migrate closer to the skin's surface, resulting in the 'bumpy' look of cellulite.

An overloaded and toxic liver and lymphatic system contribute towards cellulite problems.

Anti-Cellulite Diet:

Avoid - processed foods, artificial sweeteners, all dairy products, preserved meats and chicken. Increase the amount of raw fruits and vegetables in the diet. Use seaweeds such as kelp, arame, wakame and nori etc. Seaweeds improve thyroid function and speed up metabolism.

The following 2 recipes are excellent in reducing cellulite. Try both - you can stay with your preference, or alternate between the two.

Fat Buster

1	tomato
2	stems parsley
2	sticks celery
1	orange
1	spring onion
1	grapefruit (including pith)
1	radish
1	medium red or green pepper (capsicum) - this is not hot *

Peel the grapefruit & de-seed the pepper. Wash all ingredients, trim, chop and put through juicer. This juice can be diluted with water or cold herbal tea.

The capsicum, tomatoes, parsley and orange are all rich in bioflavonoids to support the capillaries.

Grapefruit stimulates fat metabolism

Celery helps to remove excess fluid

Metabolism Booster

1	apple (skin on), or a ripe pear
1	grapefruit - peel thinly, leaving plenty of pith
6	mint leaves
2	sticks celery

Chop fruit and put through juicer, add a dash of cinnamon (or tabasco) to serve.

Grapefruit has a high vitamin C content and is an excellent cleanser of the lymphatic system. .

Apple and mint help to eliminate toxins from the fat tissue

Celery and apple juices cleanse the subcutaneous tissues and improve kidney function.

Supplements to reduce cellulite -

Tyrosine, Vitamin B6 and the minerals zinc and chromium picolinate
Capsicum annum extract and the herb Brindleberry.

For more information on cellulite call the Dr Sandra Cabot Weight Loss Clinic on 0246558855

CHOLESTEROL PROBLEMS

Cholesterol is made up of the good HDL cholesterol and the bad LDL cholesterol. HDL cholesterol is protective against cardiovascular disease.

The most common problems we see today are -

Low blood levels of HDL cholesterol
High blood levels of LDL cholesterol
High blood levels of the fats called triglycerides

Fasting levels of the blood fats are seen below:

Fats	Normal range (in mmol/L)
Total cholesterol	3.9 to 4.5 (under 20 years of age)
Total cholesterol	3.9 to 5.5 (over 20 years of age)
Triglycerides	0.1 to 2.0
LDL cholesterol	0.5 to 3.5
HDL cholesterol	1.0 to 1.9 (males)
HDL cholesterol	1.2 to 2.3 (females)

The Ratio of $\dfrac{\text{total cholesterol}}{\text{HDL}}$ **is predictive of your risk of heart disease as follows —**

Chol/HDL ratio	RISK OF HEART DISEASE
2.5 to 3.5	below average (desirable)
3.5 to 5.5	average
5.6 to 8.3	high
> 8.3	very high

Raw Juices can save your life

Causes of abnormal blood fats -

Poor diet high in unhealthy fats such as trans-fatty acids found in margarines and hydrogenated vegetable oils. A high intake of fatty meats, full fat dairy products and deep fried foods can also elevate cholesterol levels. If the diet is high in sugar and refined carbohydrates, abnormally high levels of the fat triglyceride may develop. The combination of high triglycerides and low HDL cholesterol, is the most powerful risk factor for cardiovascular disease.

Liver dysfunction can lead to abnormal cholesterol levels, as it is the liver, which manufactures HDL and LDL cholesterol. A healthy liver keeps cholesterol levels under control. Fatty liver condition may be associated with very abnormal cholesterol levels.

Syndrome X which is the chemical imbalance that makes you store fat, is caused by a disturbance in the function of the hormone insulin. Syndrome X causes abnormalities of cholesterol and triglyceride levels. For details on a weight loss eating-plan for Syndrome X, see my new book titled "Can't Lose Weight? You could have Syndrome X - the chemical imbalance that makes you store fat"

Hereditary factors, which produce a problem in the liver's ability to regulate cholesterol production.

Juice for High Cholesterol

2	dandelion or 2 cabbage leaves
1	clove garlic or ½ red onion
1	orange
1	grapefruit
1	apple
1	radish and tops

Wash, trim and chop and pass all through the juicer. Try to leave the white pith on the citrus fruits, as it is high in bioflavonoids. Dilute with water or cold herbal tea if required.

Useful supplements and foods

Vitamin C and bioflavonoids
Lecithin
Psyllium husk powder
Oat bran
Raw nuts, seeds and cooked legumes
A good liver tonic powder or capsules

CHRONIC FATIGUE SYNDROME

Chronic fatigue is an ever-increasing problem in the community today and many people find it is difficult to find a solution. There is no doubt that raw juicing can help revitalise the immune system in such patients.

The causes of Chronic Fatigue Syndrome are -

Recurrent and/or chronic viral infections
Hidden infections in the body - *see page 45*
An imbalance of gut flora associated with infestation with unfriendly bacteria and candida.
The long term outcome of a depressive illness, which is inadequately treated
Auto-immune diseases, which must be investigated and treated
Any chronic medical illness
Liver dysfunction
Hormonal deficiencies caused by poor function of the thyroid gland and the adrenal glands
Nutritional deficiencies - in women, one of the most common underlying causes of 'that tired feeling' is iron deficiency.

It is important to strengthen the immune system and detoxify the body. This is achieved by improving the function of the liver by increasing the amount of raw vegetables in the diet and taking a powerful liver tonic in powder or capsule form.

Chlorophyll hit - for Super Energy

1	carrot
½	medium beetroot with top leaves
2	turnip leaves
1 cup	chopped parsley - must be fresh
2	spinach leaves or 2 cabbage leaves
1	medium apple - core out, skin on
½ clove	garlic or small piece ginger (optional)
1/3 cup	wheat grass (if available) - not all juicers can extract juice from wheat grass

If possible use organic produce, as pesticides can aggravate chronic fatigue.

Wash, trim, chop and pass all through juicer.

Options:

If you prefer a sweeter flavour, add 1 pear, skin on, or 1 peach (or other stone fruit) when stone fruit is in season. You can dilute with water or cold herbal tea.

Substitutes:

Dark green vegetables and their leaves are rich in chlorophyll, so you may substitute or add broccoli florets and stem, dandelion leaves, and mint to flavour. Wheat grass is excellent, as it is very high in chlorophyll (although this needs a strong juicer to pass through). Snow pea sprouts or any other sprouts with plenty of green colour are also suitable.

Beet top leaves are higher in iron than spinach but should not be taken to excess, as they have a high oxalic content and this can affect calcium metabolism.

Ginger helps improve digestion and is anti-inflammatory.

High Protein Energy Smoothie

1-cup	soymilk, almond, coconut or oat milk
1	raw organic egg
1 tbsp	whey protein powder
1 tbsp	ground flaxseeds
1	banana or ½ cup fresh berries
1	dessertspoon carob powder (optional)

Place ingredients in a blender and blend until smooth. Can add ice cubes on a hot day.

Eggs contain all the nutrients required to build cells. Make sure the eggs you use are from hormone free chickens.

Carob is a good source of calcium and protein. Its iron and copper levels help build healthy red blood cells and its magnesium helps to repair the nervous system. It is naturally sweet, unlike chocolate but has a 'chocolate-like' taste.

Soy contains phyto-estrogens, which support the hormonal system and oat milk helps to calm the nervous system.

If you suspect that hormonal imbalances are contributing towards your fatigue, ask your doctor to check the function of your thyroid and adrenal glands. In cases of adrenal gland exhaustion it may be necessary to use hormone replacement therapy with DHEA, natural testosterone or pregnenelone. These hormones are available in cream or lozenge form. Replacement with these hormones can make a huge difference to those with chronic fatigue syndrome.

Important nutritional supplements are -

A magnesium supplement containing a combination of -
- Magnesium orotate
- Magnesium aspartate
- Magnesium amino acid chelate
- Magnesium phosphate

A tablet containing selenium, vitamin E and C and zinc.

Co-enzyme Q10 can increase energy production in the body

A good liver tonic powder can be added to the juices

COLDS AND FLU

Colds and flues are caused by infection with respiratory or influenza viruses and are highly contagious. Colds are often the body's way of detoxifying itself. Fevers are the natural defence the body uses to make its internal terrain unfriendly towards invading bacteria and viruses. In adults, fevers, unless very high, should not be interfered with, but rather supported, so allowing the body to cleanse itself. In children high fevers can result in convulsions and must be controlled. Often the best way of bringing down a childhood fever is to bathe the child in a tepid bath.

Concentrated foods such as refined carbohydrates, meats, dairy products and sugars can all have the potential to increase the body's load of toxins. Support of the body's cleansing mechanisms can be achieved by juicing and not eating for a day or so, while the body rids itself of the overload of toxins.

Increased hydration is essential and raw juices and water can help the cleansing process. Increased amounts of vitamin C are needed during these infections.

Cold and Flu Juice number one

2	lemons - juiced
1	clove garlic
1/2cm	slice fresh ginger root
1	apple, core out, skin on
1	pear, core out, skin on
1cup	hot water
1 tbsp	honey or more, to your taste

In adults a 2 cm slice of horseradish can be added if desired

Options:-

If the juice is not to your liking - divide the recipe into 2 separate combinations

1.   lemon, garlic, ginger, water and honey
2.   lemon, apple, pear, water and honey

Dissolve honey in hot water, juice all the other ingredients and add juice to water and honey. This is excellent for adults and children.

Lemon is included as a mainstay of this recipe because of its high vitamin C content. It has natural antiseptic properties.

Apple contains pectin, which helps to remove harmful substances from the intestines.

Garlic contains allicin, which helps fight infection and is a natural antibiotic.

Ginger has natural antibiotic properties and reduces mucous congestion.

Horseradish breaks up and removes mucous plugs.

Cold and Flu Juice number two

¼ tsp	ground aniseed
2	lemons - juiced
2 slices	pineapple
1 tbsp	honey
Sprinkle	cinnamon or cayenne pepper
1-cup	hot water

Steep aniseed in hot water for 5 minutes and strain. Then juice and add other ingredients. Sip slowly. This juice will help with problems of congestion.

Pineapple is rich in bromelain, which helps to break up foreign microbes and catarrh.

Cayenne has an antiseptic and cleansing action

Cinnamon is an astringent and reduces mucous discharges.

Helpful supplements -

Vital C powder in a dose of ½ tsp twice daily.

Some studies have shown that taking Vitamin C, especially in daily doses of 1 gram or over, has the potential to lessen the intensity of colds and flu.

Olive leaf extract capsules in a dose of 1000mg three times daily with food, or Olive leaf extract in elixir form in children. All children should be assessed by a doctor to exclude serious causes of fever such as meningitis, which can be rapidly fatal.

CONSTIPATION

Eating large amounts of cooked and processed foods can contribute to sluggish bowels. Over a period of time, a layer of toxic waste products may build up on the lining of the sluggish bowel. This build-up can cause inflammation in the bowel, and the toxins are absorbed from the bowel and travel back to the liver via the portal vein. The liver has to work much harder to break down these internally produced toxins and symptoms of liver dysfunction may result. Thus constipation can lead to headaches, abdominal bloating, fatigue, allergies and skin problems.

Regular daily well-formed bowel movements without straining should be normal. This reduces the risk of conditions such as appendicitis, hiatus hernia, abdominal hernias, haemorrhoids and colonic cancer. If the bowel moves as often as food is eaten, say 2 to 3 times a day, this can help reduce a build-up of toxic waste products in the bowel.

Common causes of constipation are -

A diet deficient in fibre and/or raw fruits and vegetables.

Lack of exercise

Dehydration with inadequate intake of water.

Abuse of laxatives or drug side effects.

Underactivity of the thyroid gland.

Mechanical problems with the bowel are common, such as prolapsed bowel or extra loops of bowel or bowel pockets. These pockets form in the wall of the colon and this condition is called diverticulitis. These conditions can only be diagnosed with a barium enema X-ray and colonoscopy.

The following juice can help to reduce the toxic load in the bowel by encouraging elimination and regular bowel actions.

Constipation Juice

2	spinach leaves or 2 dandelion leaves or 2 cabbage leaves
1	green apple, skin on
100g	dried prunes - stones removed
100g	figs - fresh if in season, otherwise dried
50g	fresh rhubarb
50g	fresh cherries (stones removed) - this is optional

Wash all fresh ingredients and chop to fit juicer intake. Soak dried fruits in water overnight then pass through juicer with all other ingredients.

Options:

Dilute with water to your taste, as the extra water will help the bowels.
You can substitute stone fruits in season and also berries to make up same amounts.

Apple fibre and pectin soothes the intestines and reduces constipation.

Cherries contain magnesium, which aids contractions of the muscle in the walls of the bowel.

Spinach is high in cleansing chlorophyll.

Prunes are high in fibre and soften the stool for easy passage

Figs are high in fibre and have a laxative effect. Those with diverticulitis may need to avoid figs, as their seeds can become trapped in the bowel pockets.

Useful supplements -

FibreTone powder - 1 to 2 tbsp with breakfast
Ground flaxseed - 1 to 2 tbsp with breakfast
Metamucil or Normacol

CYSTITIS AND KIDNEY PROBLEMS

Cystitis means inflammation of the bladder and may be sudden in onset (acute) or chronic (longstanding).

Inflammation and infection can travel upwards from the bladder and eventually affect the kidneys, which is called pyelonephritis.

Raw Juices can save your life

It is important to get bladder infections under control quickly, as continued episodes increase the likelihood of infection involving the upper urinary tract and the kidneys, which can result in permanent scarring of the kidneys.

Causes of urinary tract infections -

Infection with bacteria, which often originate from bacteria in the bowel or vagina. This can be aggravated by poor personal hygiene, and mechanical problems such as urinary reflux from the bladder or prolapse of the vagina or bowel.

Sexual intercourse can aggravate or trigger bladder infections - this is sometimes called "honeymoon cystitis".

Inadequate hydration can cause stagnation of urine. Stagnant urine becomes infected more easily.

A poor diet, which is lacking in raw foods and antioxidants.

Hormonal deficiencies of oestrogen and testosterone, which are common in menopausal women. These deficiencies result in thinning (atrophy) of the tissues of the vagina and bladder thus making them more fragile and vulnerable to infection.

Immune dysfunction which can result in auto-immune diseases such as nephritis (inflammation of the kidney). Immune dysfunction can also result in chronic inflammation of the entire bladder wall and this painful condition is known as chronic interstitial cystitis.

Stones forming in the bladder, ureters and kidneys, which obstruct the free flow of urine, thus increasing the risk of infection.

Juice for the urinary tract

½ cup	fresh cranberries
2 stems	celery
1	medium apple, skin on
½	grapefruit
1/2 to 1	clove garlic or ½ red onion
1	small Lebanese cucumber
1	medium carrot
1	small red radish & top leaves

Wash all ingredients, chop and push through juicer.

Options:

Leave out the garlic or onion, if the juice is not to your liking.

Add ½ beetroot, 3 large strawberries or more apples for a sweeter taste if preferred. You can dilute with water or cold herbal tea.

The inclusion of cranberries in this juice can help to prevent bacteria from adhering to the lining of the bladder and urethra. If the bacteria cannot adhere to the mucosa, they are unable to cause infection.

The garlic has antimicrobial activity against bacteria such as E.coli and Staphylococcus, which are associated with urinary tract infections.

Cucumber has an anti-inflammatory effect on the urinary tract.

Radish is a natural antibiotic with anti-inflammatory properties.

Carrot contains high quantities of beta-carotene, which is essential for healthy mucous membranes.

Apple has the ability to soothe the mucous membranes.

Celery acts as a diuretic to enhance urine flow.

Note:

It is vital that those with infections or diseases of the urinary tract increase their intake of water to 2 to 3 litres daily. Raw juicing is absolutely imperative and must become a way of life. Kidney disease is very common and is often present for years before being detected. This is unfortunate, as permanent damage to the kidneys may have already occurred which can be difficult to reverse. It is important to have your urine checked regularly if you have bladder or kidney problems. Indeed a mid-stream sample of urine can be checked every 3 months to detect problems at an early and treatable stage.

Useful supplements -

Selenium, zinc and magnesium.

Vitamin C powder - this should be taken everyday to keep the urine slightly acidic - you can experiment to find the most effective dose of vitamin C. You will need between 500 to 2000mg daily, which is best taken in 3 divided doses. Some people will find that ascorbic acid is too irritating, and may be better with the ascorbate or ester C forms of vitamin C.

Olive leaf extract capsules or elixir can be taken daily in a dose of 1000 to 2000mg daily. For acute infections it is necessary to increase the dose of olive leaf to 1000mg three times daily.

These supplements and raw juices can act as natural antibiotics which is important, as infecting bacteria often become resistant to antibiotic drugs which are used long term.

Hormone replacement therapy with natural oestrogen, progesterone and testosterone may enable urinary tract infections to be well controlled in peri-menopausal women. Creams containing combinations of these hormones can be applied to the vagina and vulval areas on a nightly basis. They are best used at night after sexual intercourse and after you have emptied your bladder and are ready to go to sleep.

DEEP VEIN THROMBOSIS - *see Varicose Veins page138*

DEPRESSION

Depression is a common problem in today's world and continues to be a major cause of personal suffering and lost productivity. Many persons suffering with depression do not seek effective treatment, as they fail to recognise that they are depressed.

Causes of depression -
Chemical imbalances in the neuro-transmitters in the brain - this is known as endogenous depression

Loss of the important things in life such as - loss of money, employment, status, health, youth and relationships etc.

Stress and work overload

Hormonal imbalances such as premenstrual syndrome, menopause and post natal depression

Symptoms of depression -
Unhappiness and sadness

Feeling flat with loss of highs and lows

Loss of enthusiasm for life

Broken sleep

Loss of self esteem
Excessively guilty feelings
Reclusive behaviour
Inability to concentrate and poor memory

Juice for Depression Number One

6	strawberries or 1 small bunch grapes
1 cup	chopped broccoli
1	carrot
6	string beans
2	lettuce leaves

Wash, trim and chop and pass through the juicer.

Juice for Depression Number Two

2	large spinach leaves
2	stems celery
2-3	lettuce leaves
1	medium beetroot & tops.
1 cup	grapes or 1 medium carrot
1	tomato (vine-ripened or organic is best)
A dash	of Tabasco sauce (optional)

Wash, trim and chop and process through juicer. Approximately ½ litre can be taken daily.

Options:-

Cucumber can also be added as this has a calming effect.

Celery is high in magnesium, which helps to calm the nervous system.

Beetroot contains magnesium and calcium for the nervous system, chromium to maintain balanced blood sugar levels and iron to support the manufacture of red blood cells.

Carrot contains calcium, potassium, magnesium and B vitamins. This helps to promote a balanced nervous system.

Lettuce contains a natural sedative called lactucarium, which helps to calm the nervous system.

Tabasco contains cayenne or chilli, which releases endorphins from the brain. These are the natural happy chemicals produced by the brain and help to lift the mood and reduce pain.

Useful supplements and foods -
Magnesium
St Johns Wort (hypericum)
B - group vitamins
The amino acid tyrosine
Essential fatty acids - flaxseed oil, primrose oil & oily fish

**For more information call the
Health Advisory Service on 02 4655 8855**

DIABETES

Those who suffer with diabetes will benefit from increasing the amount of vegetables in the diet and juicing raw vegetables. Those who suffer with diabetes type I are better to avoid fruit juices and eat the whole fruit instead.

Diabetes type II is associated with poor function of the hormone insulin and these patients exhibit insulin resistance and may have excessively high levels of insulin. If diabetes type II is detected in the early stages, while the body is still producing its own insulin, it can often be completely reversed. The chemical imbalance of Syndrome X often leads to diabetes type II and can be helped with the same strategies. For a good eating plan for Syndrome X and diabetes type II, see my new book titled **"Can't Lose Weight? You could have Syndrome X** - *the chemical imbalance that makes you store fat"*

Juice for Diabetes Number One

½ tsp	fenugreek seed powder
¼ cup	hot water.
¼	Bitter melon (if available)
1	carrot
2	dandelion leaves or 2 cabbage leaves
1	spring onion

4	string beans or 2 Brussels sprouts
½ cup	chopped fennel
¼ cup	chopped parsley including stems
2	stems celery with top leaves
1/2	clove garlic (optional)

Pour hot water over fenugreek powder. Allow to steep 15 minutes.

Wash and chop all other ingredients and put through juicer. Add to fenugreek mix. (If preferred, the water may be drained off and used without the fenugreek residue, but this could reduce the beneficial properties of the drink)

Options:

Diabetics will know how much sugar they can tolerate at one time. If you would like to add any fruits to temper the taste of this vegetable juice, you need to err on the side of caution. The best fruits are - apples, oranges, grapefruits, cherries and plums. It is quite acceptable to dilute the juices used for diabetes type 2 or Syndrome X (1 part juice to 1 part water).

Garlic is known to have a significant effect in lowering blood-sugar levels.

Bitter melon (Momordica charantia), also known as Balsam pear, is a tropical vegetable, commonly grown in Asia. Indigenous peoples have used its juice for centuries to lower blood sugar levels. It has insulin-like properties, which have been shown in some clinical studies to have beneficial results in the regulation of blood sugar.

Dandelion and cabbage leaves act as a liver tonic. The liver plays a vital role in regulating blood sugar levels.

String beans are rich in potassium, which is essential for pancreatic function.

Fennel and fenugreek are beneficial for the pancreas and liver.

Juice for Diabetes Number Two

8	green string beans
2	Brussels sprouts
1	carrot
¼ cup	chopped fennel (can include green tips)
2	spinach leaves

Note: The juice of Brussels sprouts when combined with carrot, string beans and spinach, provides a combination of properties, which strengthen and regenerate the pancreas. The pancreas produces insulin and needs to be supported in diabetes and Syndrome X. This juice is very potent so you may dilute with water or cold herbal tea.

Useful supplements -

The herbs - Gymnema Sylvestre and Bitter melon
Carnitine fumarate or L -carnitine
The minerals - chromium picolinate, selenium, magnesium, manganese, and zinc.
Lipoic acid

These can be taken individually, or combined together in supplement form.

All diabetics must remain under the close supervision of their own doctor.

DIARRHOEA - *see IBS page 110 and IBD page 105*

DIGESTIVE PROBLEMS

Digestive problems can result in -

Abdominal pain and discomfort, after eating.
Abdominal bloating after eating.
Fatigue and headaches after eating.
Nausea and poor appetite.
Bad breath and coated tongue.
Vomiting.

Gastric reflux and heartburn causing pain behind the breast bone.
Peptic ulcers.
Nutritional deficiencies due to poor absorption of nutrients.

Causes of digestive problems -

Stress from lifestyle choices and family/work problems.
Food allergies or intolerances.
Inadequate production of digestive enzymes from the pancreas.
Inadequate production of hydrochloric acid and pepsin from the stomach.
Unfriendly bacteria in the stomach and small intestines, such as candida and helicobacter pylori infection.
Hiatus hernia of the stomach.
Side effects from drugs.

Infection with Helicobacter pylori bacterium

The Helicobacter pylori bacterium infects the mucus lining of the stomach. This bacteria causes inflammation of the lining of the stomach and duodenum, which can result in peptic ulcers. Some people with the infection have no symptoms, but others report nausea, bad breath, excess gas, bloating and a burning stomach pain. Helicobacter pylori is passed in the stool and contact infection is thought to be acquired through unwashed hands, contaminated foods and water. Because of the method of transmission whole families often have this gut infection. The juice recipes below will provide high levels of enzymes to assist the breakdown and absorption of nutrients.

Juice number one

To assist peptic ulcers, gastritis, heartburn and gastro-oesophageal reflux

1	large red apple with skin on, OR 1 large pear with skin on
2	stems celery
1 cup	alfalfa sprouts
1	medium carrot
1 to 2	large cabbage leaves (*Chinese cabbage very suitable*)
1	Handful seeded black cherries

Raw Juices can save your life

Wash, chop and juice all ingredients. Drink 1 cup twice daily. Dilute with 50% water if you find the juice too strong. Add 1 tbsp of Aloe Vera juice and/or acidophilus powder if desired for extra benefit.

Cabbage is known for its powerful healing properties on the gut.

Apples contain pectin, which has soothing properties.

Pears assist digestion and are very good for those with food allergies.

Cherries help regulate the production of digestive juices.

Carrot juice is high in beta-carotene, which heals the mucous membranes.

Juice number two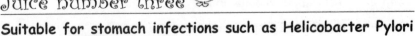

To assist weak digestion

1/3	pineapple, skin on
1	orange or ½ grapefruit
1/3	cucumber
1	apple skin on
2	slices pawpaw
1-tsp	honey, or a tiny pinch of stevia powder (stevia is a natural sweetener)

Pawpaw and pineapple contain natural digestive enzymes such as papain and bromelain.

Cucumber contains erepsin, an enzyme that helps to digest proteins.

Trim the rough, dry pieces from pineapple but retain as much green as you can. Thinly peel citrus leaving as much pith as possible. Wash all ingredients and pass through the juicer. Add honey or stevia to the juice. Drink twice a day, half an hour before meals.

Juice number three

Suitable for stomach infections such as Helicobacter Pylori

¼	pineapple (peeled)
½ cup	chopped cauliflower with stem & leaf
½ cup	watercress
2	cabbage leaves (green)
1	red radish with top leaves
½ to 1	clove garlic (optional)
1	pomegranate (when in season) - seeds & flesh

Wash, chop and put all through juicer. Drink 1 cup twice daily, or more frequently if helpful. You may dilute with water or cold herbal tea.

Options:

1 medium carrot or 1 medium apple may be added for sweeter flavour.

Ginger is a natural remedy to settle the digestion and also addresses nausea.

Radish is a natural antibiotic and supports liver function.

Pomegranate reduces intestinal parasites such as worms, amoeba, giardia and helicobacter pylori.

Juice number four

Suitable to reduce gas and abdominal bloating

1	cabbage leaf
1 cm	slice fresh ginger root - can use less if this is too potent
3	slices fresh pineapple - can use more if needed
4 to 6	mint leaves

Wash, chop and put all through juicer. Drink 1 cup twice daily, or more frequently if helpful.

"Smoothie" for Peptic Ulcers

This is a drink mixture that is best prepared in a blender.

1	ripe banana
1	apple or 1 small bunch dark grapes [seedless]
4	strawberries
1 tbsp	slippery elm powder (can use less if desired)
1 cup	oat milk or coconut milk

If appetite is poor add 1 tbsp whey protein powder

Wash, trim and chop and process all in blender until smooth

Useful foods and supplements -

Digestive enzymes can be taken with every meal, such as Pancreatin or Pancrease. The most effective enzymes contain pancreas extract. A small glass of water containing a tbsp of apple cider vinegar and 1 tsp honey can be sipped slowly during each meal.

Chia seed can heal an ulcerated inflamed gut - there are several ways to take it. It can be soaked in water overnight and eaten cold or warmed with oat milk. Refer to the book titled "The Magic of Chia" by James Scheer, published by Frog Ltd. Berkeley California

L - glutamine, which can be taken as a powder, to heal the lining of the stomach.

FLUID RETENTION

Fluid retention can be caused by -

Hormonal imbalances such as an under active thyroid gland.
Taking the oral contraceptive pill or potent hormone replacement therapy
Kidney problems
Sluggish liver function.
Liver disease.
Heart disease and heart failure.
Problems with the lymphatic system.
Varicose veins, which cause fluid retention in the legs,

Fluid retention is made worse by poor diet, lack of exercise and taking artificial sweeteners.

The diuretic juice on page 86 will also aid high blood pressure problems, and the often-associated kidney dysfunction, which results in oedema.

Diuretic juice

1/4 cup	chopped parsley
2	dandelion leaves or ½ cup chopped watercress leaves
2	stems celery, leaves on
½ cm	fresh ginger root
1	red radish with tops
1	Lebanese cucumber - skin on
1	orange
8 -10	fresh mint leaves

Wash, chop and put all ingredients through juicer.

Options:

If you want a sweeter flavour, add some fresh pineapple or an extra orange. You may dilute with water or cold herbal tea.

Cucumber's potassium content helps to regulate blood pressure, whether high or low. It supports kidney function and has diuretic properties.

Radish, celery, dandelion and parsley are natural diuretics.

Vitamin C and bioflavonoids are able to reduce swelling of the limbs and improve kidney function. The white pith of citrus fruits is replete with bioflavonoids.

Vitamins C and B, and the minerals, potassium and magnesium, are important in regulating kidney function. Parsley, celery, cucumber and radish supply these essential nutrients.

Useful supplements -

Magnesium, Vitamin C and bioflavonoids. The herbs "butcher's broom" and "horsechestnut".

Buckwheat contains valuable rutin to strengthen the veins and lymphatic vessels.

ENDOMETRIOSIS

This common gynaecological condition is caused when the uterine lining (endometrium) grows outside the uterine cavity in abnormal positions such as the pelvic and abdominal cavities. The uterine lining is normally confined within the uterus, from where it is shed every month in the form of the menstrual bleed. Unfortunately this bleeding also occurs in the abnormally situated endometrium, resulting in internal bleeding and scarring. The uterine tubes (fallopian tubes) often become blocked resulting in infertility.

Symptoms that may be produced by endometriosis -

    Painful menstrual bleeding
    Heavy menstrual bleeding with blood clots
    Infertility
    Abdominal and pelvic pain may become permanent
    Abdominal bloating
    Painful sexual intercourse

Causes of endometriosis

    Immune dysfunction
    Poor diet deficient in raw foods and antioxidants
    Hormonal imbalances such as a deficiency of progesterone
    Genetic factors

Endometriosis Juice

1	Carrot
½ cup	chopped wheat grass (if available)
1 cm	slice of fresh ginger root
½ cup	coriander leaves
¼	medium-sized pineapple
1	whole orange or grapefruit
2	very dark green spinach leaves
¼ cup	parsley

Wash, trim and chop ingredients. Remove rough, dry pieces from pineapple but retain some skin. Put all ingredients through juicer. Drink 1 cup, 2 to 3 times daily. Store covered in refrigerator up to 24 hours.

Options:

Make up 1 cup of orange & wattle seed tea - cool and add to juices, to dilute the juice if preferred. If you dilute, you may be able to increase the wheat grass up to one full cup.

Pineapple contains enzymes, which help to break up blood clots and scar tissue.

The essential oil in Coriander relieves gas, and reduces intestinal cramps.

Wheat grass is a cleanser, and like all the other green leafy vegetables in this juice, supplies vitamin K. Vitamin K helps to reduce excessive bleeding. Wheat grass also contains zinc, which helps to reduce adhesions.

Carrot contains betacarotene, which reduces inflammation.

Citrus contains vitamin C to reduce inflammation and heavy bleeding.

Ginger contains natural anti-inflammatory substances.

Helpful supplements -

Vitamin E

Selenium and zinc

Essential fatty acids - cold pressed flaxseed oil and primrose oil

Avoid all dairy products, and meats that are produced with hormones.

ECZEMA - *see skin problems page 131*

EYE PROBLEMS

Common problems affecting the eyes are -

Presbyopia, which results in the need to wear glasses at some time after the age of 40

Clouding of the lens (cataract)

Degeneration of the back of the eye (retina), the most common form being macular degeneration

Eye strain

Increased pressure in the eye (glaucoma)

Raw Juices can save your life

Detachment of the back of the eye (retinal detachment)
Haemorrhage or blood clots in the eyes

Common causes of eye problems -

Computers, fluorescent lights and pollution
Dehydration
Smoking
Excessive use of alcohol and caffeine
Diabetes
High blood pressure
Immune dysfunction
Infections of the eyes with viruses or bacteria
Poor circulation (atherosclerosis)
Poor diet with deficiency of raw foods and antioxidants

Raw juicing can help all of the above eye problems. Avoid smoking and high intakes of caffeine and alcohol. Diabetes and blood pressure must be carefully controlled to protect the eyes.

Eye Juice number one

1 cup chopped parsley
1 carrot
2 fresh apricots (if in season)
1 whole spring onion or 1 clove garlic
1 stick celery
1 medium beetroot
1 dandelion or cabbage leaf

Wash, trim, chop and juice - drink 1 to 2 cups per day.

Parsley is high in vitamin C, which is an antioxidant for the eyes.
Spring onions contain vitamin B and zinc, both essential for healthy eyes.
Carrot, apricots and dandelion have excellent levels of betacarotene, which protects the eyes.

Eye Juice number two

1	carrot
1	medium beetroot and tops
2	dandelion leaves (if available)
1	whole orange
1	grapefruit - thinly peel rind but leave pith
2	spinach leaves
½ to 1	clove garlic (optional)

Wash, trim and chop. Pass all through the juicer. Drink 1 to 2 cups daily. You can dilute with water or cold herbal tea.

Carrots, dandelion, and beetroot can help to restore night vision.
Grapefruit and orange are high in vitamin C, which reduces the risk of cataracts.
Spinach is high in chlorophyll, which has antioxidant properties for the eyes.
Garlic thins the blood and improves circulation to the eyes.

Useful supplements
The herbs ginkgo biloba, horsechestnut and bilberry
The minerals selenium, zinc and magnesium
Lipoic acid
Essential fatty acids such as cold pressed flaxseed and evening primrose oil
Vitamins C and E

FIBROMYALGIA

Fibromyalgia is a very common problem, which presents as pain and tenderness in the muscles and connective tissues. There is often a deep aching pain in the muscles and ligaments and it may also affect the joints. The pain of fibromyalgia commonly affects the neck and shoulders but may also affect the muscles of the back and limbs. It is commonly associated with stiffness and sufferers usually have tender points in the affected areas. Women are more commonly affected, and fibromyalgia often begins during the peri-menopausal years. Fibromyalgia is often associated with chronic fatigue and headaches.

Causes of fibromyalgia -

Immune dysfunction with excessive inflammation

Autoimmune diseases such as lupus.

Post-viral syndrome

Chronic trauma to the tissues from injuries

Hormonal imbalances with deficiencies of oestrogen, progesterone, testosterone and DHEA

Adrenal gland exhaustion

Deficiencies of minerals such as magnesium and selenium

In fibromyalgia there appears to be a dysfunction in the muscle cells, which causes a loss of magnesium and potassium from inside the cells, and an accumulation of calcium. The calcium excess, causes small fibres of muscle to contract, forming nodules or fibrous bands in the muscles. There is an increase in lactic acid levels in the affected muscle and pain develops.

Fibromyalgia Juice

1	carrot
2	small Lebanese or 1/2 Continental cucumber
3	sticks celery
½ cm	fresh root ginger
3	slices pineapple

Wash, trim, chop and process in juicer. Drink 1 cup or 250 ml, twice daily.

The above juice will supply plenty of minerals and also exerts an anti-inflammatory effect. This juice also helps to reduce acidity in the muscles and joints.

Useful supplements

A comprehensive Bone and Joint nutrient capsule containing -

Glucosamine sulphate, calcium hydroxyapatite, vitamin D, manganese, magnesium, zinc, selenium, copper and horsetail (to provide silica).

Essential fatty acids - cold pressed flaxseed oil, salmon oil and evening primrose oil.

Hormone Replacement Therapy (HRT) consisting of combinations of natural oestrogen, testosterone, pregnenolone and DHEA may produce good relief of pain and stiffness.

For more information call the Health Advisory Service on 02 4655 8855

FLATULENCE (Intestinal Gas)

This embarrassing condition results from excessive formation of gas in the intestines and may result in burping and/or release of gas from the anus. It is often associated with abdominal bloating and discomfort and irregular bowel actions.

Causes of flatulence -

Unfriendly micro-organisms such as bacteria, parasites and fungi, growing in the stomach and intestines. This condition is called dysbiosis. These unhealthy micro-organisms cause fermentation of stagnant food in the intestines resulting in intestinal gas.

Inflammation of the bowel from ulcerative colitis or Crohn's disease

Bowel pockets known as diverticulitis

Redundant bowel caused by excessive loops of enlarged bowel

Excessive use of antibiotic drugs and cortisone

Poor dietary choices with excess consumption of processed foods and preserved meats, and a lack of raw foods in the diet.

Anti-gas Juice

100gm	chopped cabbage or Brussels sprouts
1	red radish
1	clove garlic (excellent for gut infections) - optional
1 cup	chopped fennel
1/3 cup	coriander leaves, chopped
1	apple
1	pear

You may need more cabbage depending on how juicy it is. Wash, trim and chop, and process all in juicer. Drink 3 small glasses, 30 minutes before meals.

Note: If you find that the cabbage initially increases the level of flatulence, you may need to water down the cabbage juice (½ juice to ½ water).

Useful supplements -

Use supplements of friendly bacteria such as acidophilus and lactobacillus

Plain acidophilus yogurt

Peppermint tea

Digestive enzymes such as pancreatin or pancrease (should contain pancreas extract)

A good liver tonic powder to stimulate the flow of healthy bile

A powder to ease the colon containing a combination of the following ingredients -

> Glutamine
>
> Lactobacillus acidophilus
>
> Fructo-oligosaccharides
>
> Pectin
>
> Glucosamine sulphate
>
> Slippery elm & Fennel

GALLSTONES AND BILIARY PROBLEMS

Problems with the gall bladder and biliary system are very common and consist of -

Inflammation of the gall bladder and bile ducts

Muscular spasms and/or poor contraction of the gall bladder wall

Stones forming in the gall bladder and/or bile ducts

Obstruction to the free flow of bile

Causes of gall bladder and biliary dysfunction-

Production of toxic bile by the liver

Inadequate production of bile by the liver

Sluggish flow of bile

Excess amounts of cholesterol in the bile resulting in stone formation

Infection of the gall bladder

Poor dietary choices with excess consumption of fatty foods, dairy products and fried foods.

The hormonal changes of pregnancy

The oral contraceptive pill and some types of hormone replacement therapy

Some types of blood disorders

Symptoms of gall bladder dysfunction -

Indigestion and nausea after eating (especially fatty foods)

Vomiting attacks

Pain in the right upper abdomen, which often radiates to the right shoulder and back.

Gall Bladder Juice number one

2	fresh dandelion leaves
1	medium carrot
3cm	slice beetroot
1	medium apple
2	cabbage leaves or 2 Brussels sprouts
2	turnip leaves
1	large ripe tomato whole

Wash, trim and chop and process all in juicer. For variety and to enhance the flavour, you may add a small grapefruit, a little watercress, or a small radish. You may dilute with water or cold herbal tea.

Useful supplements -

A good liver tonic powder containing -

St Mary's Thistle

Sulphur bearing amino acids - taurine, glutamine & cysteine

Glycine, B - group vitamins, anti-oxidants, and lecithin

MSM and vitamin C powder - ½ tsp daily

Drink 2 to 3 litres of water daily and eat plenty of raw vegetables. Avoid dairy products, and deep-fried or fatty foods.

HAEMORRHOIDS

Haemorrhoids are swollen veins (varicose veins) situated in the lower bowel (rectum and anus).

 Raw Juices can save your life

Causes of haemorrhoids -

Liver congestion or liver disease
Constipation
Prolonged straining during a bowel action
Poor diet deficient in raw foods, fibre and water
Pregnancy
Alcohol abuse

Anti-haemorrhoid Juice

1 cup	chopped watercress or 2 cabbage leaves or 2 turnip leaves
1	large carrot
2-3	large spinach leaves & stems, or 2 dandelion leaves
1	clove garlic or ½ small red onion
1	grapefruit or 1 orange with white outside skin (pith) left on

Wash, trim and chop then process through juicer. Drink one glass twice daily.

Prune juice may also be drunk at breakfast to improve bowel habits. Soak dried prunes in water overnight, take out stones and juice the fruit. You may drink it by itself, or add it to the anti-haemorrhoid juice. You may also dilute juice with water, as increased fluid intake is vital to overcome haemorrhoids.

Useful supplements and foods

Ground flaxseed - 1 to 2 tbsp daily, with breakfast cereal - use a food processor or coffee grinder, or buy in packets (must be fresh or it can be rancid).
Psyllium seed powder
FibreTone powder OR Normacol powder
Buckwheat & fresh wheatgerm
Apple cider vinegar - 1 to 2 tbsp daily in 1 glass water - add honey and sip slowly during meals
Vitamin E
Vitamin C and bioflavonoids

HAIRLOSS

Hair loss is a common problem and often causes great psychological distress. It may occur in -

A small area of the scalp

In the male pattern of baldness (fronto-temporal areas of the scalp)

All over the scalp and indeed sometimes all the body hair may be lost

Causes of hair loss

Stress

Immune dysfunction and auto-immune diseases such as lupus or alopecia

Trauma to the scalp

Side effects of Chemotherapy or other prescription drugs

Hormonal disorders -

Thyroid gland dysfunction

Pregnancy and post natal period

Menopause

Excessive male hormones

Note: all these hormonal disorders can be checked for with a blood test

Hereditary factors especially in men

Ageing

Overdosing with vitamin A

Fungal infections of the scalp

Juice to thicken the hair

1-cup	alfalfa sprouts
2	cabbage leaves or 2 Brussels sprouts
1-cup	broccoli florets
1	medium carrot
2	slices red onion
1	medium beetroot and tops
½ to 1	clove garlic (optional)
2	slices of watermelon (to sweeten if desired)

Wash, trim and chop, and process through juicer.

 Raw Juices can save your life

Cabbage, broccoli, Brussels sprouts, onion and garlic are high in organic sulphur, which stimulates the growth of healthy hair.

Alfalfa in its sprouted form is a valuable source of phyto-estrogens, which help to counteract the effect of excessive male hormones on the hair follicles.

Silicon rich foods such as alfalfa and onion, help the growth of strong and healthy hair.

Carrot, broccoli and beetroot contain beta-carotene essential to reduce inflammation in the scalp.

Garlic contains selenium, which reduces inflammation in the scalp.

This juice will also improve the circulation of oxygen rich blood to the scalp.

Useful foods and supplements -

Selenium and zinc to reduce dandruff and fungal infections of the scalp.

MSM and vitamin C powder to supply organic sulphur and improve circulation to the scalp.

Essential fatty acids such as flaxseed oil, salmon oil and evening primrose oil.

Vitamin E to reduce scarring of the hair follicles and improve the circulation.

Hormone therapy - Natural progesterone can help to thicken the hair and is available in the form of creams or lozenges (troches).

Anti-male hormones such as Androcur (cyproterone acetate) available in tablet form. Androcur can be used in women with excessive male hormones, which can occur in polycystic ovarian syndrome or during the peri-menopause.

For more information call the Health Advisory Service on 0246558855.

HANGOVER

The morning after the night before can be a real headache - literally! The liver has to process alcohol and large amounts of alcohol will cause acute inflammation of the liver.

Typical symptoms of a hangover are -

Nausea and vomiting
Diarrhoea
Headaches which may be severe
Dehydration
Foggy brain syndrome

Hangover Recovery Juice

1	medium carrot
1	medium apple, skin on
2	slices watermelon, with some white pith
1	medium orange
1	medium grapefruit (unless you cannot cope with the slightly acid taste)
2cm	slice beetroot
2	fresh dandelion leaves or 2 cabbage leaves

Wash, trim and chop, and pass through the juicer. Drink 1 small glass on retiring. Drink another when you wake up, and continue to drink small glasses (100 to 200mls) every hour. Make sure that you drink plenty of pure water as well.

This juice will -

Support and improve liver function
Reduce inflammation of the stomach
Hydrate the body
Reduce nausea
Boost energy levels
Reduce the headache of hangover

Helpful supplements -

A liver tonic powder can be added to the juice - ½ tsp with every glass of juice
Magnesium helps to reduce the headache
B vitamins support the liver
Grated apple helps to settle an acid stomach

HAY FEVER - *see Sinus page 130*

HEART PROBLEMS

Heart disease is the leading cause of death in modern day society and is increasing because of the ageing population. Many people with heart disease will be on medications to control blood pressure, blood clotting and the muscular action of the heart. These drugs can be life saving and can control angina pain, heart failure and cardiac arrhythmia (palpitations). Even if you are dependent upon medications, raw juicing can help to reduce the risk factors for heart disease and also provide antioxidants to protect the blood vessels and the heart muscle.

If you have heart disease it is vital to control your blood pressure and cholesterol and triglyceride levels, and to keep your weight in the healthy range.

The most common types of heart disease are -

Coronary artery blockage (atherosclerosis of the arteries supplying the heart with blood). This commonly leads to angina (heart pain) and heart attacks (myocardial infarction).

Heart failure due to weakening of the heart muscle

Diseases of the heart valves

Inflammation of the heart muscle (cardiomyopathy) due to viral infections or auto-immune disease

Juice for heart disease number one

3	sticks celery
½ cup	red or black berries
1	tomato (organic or vine-ripened is best)
1	grapefruit
1	red onion
1	clove garlic (optional)

Wash, trim and chop all ingredients and pass through juicer. Dilute if preferred.

Juice for heart disease number 2

1	carrot
1	turnip
1	spring onion
2	dandelion leaves
1	red capsicum
1	orange
1	leek

Wash, trim and chop all ingredients and pass through juicer. Dilute if preferred.

Useful Supplements - to be used only after your doctor's consent

Magnesium, zinc and selenium

Vitamin E

Vitamin C and bioflavonoids

Flaxseed oil - cold pressed

HEADACHES

Headaches are a common problem and are generally transient and eased by a mild analgesic such as tablets containing a combination of paracetamol or aspirin with codeine. Sometimes they can be relieved simply by lying down at the first hint of a headache in a dark room, drinking cool water and placing a cold pack over the head and face. The causes of headaches are almost too numerous to mention, however you can see from the long list of causes below, that the cause can be sinister. Thus it is important that you see your doctor for tests to exclude serious causes of headaches. This is particularly so if the headaches are constant, severe or frequent in nature.

Required tests may include -

CAT scans of the head and neck

Blood tests to check the immune system, liver and kidney function, hormonal levels and a full blood count.

A thorough general physical examination is required and a check up from a specialist neurologist is essential in cases of severe headaches.

Causes of headaches

Dehydration

Fever and systemic infections

Substance abuse with caffeine, cigarettes or alcohol - see hangover juice *page 97*

Stress and anxiety causing muscle spasm in the head and neck

Neck problems and fibromyalgia

Immune dysfunction causing inflammation in the blood vessels, muscles and connective tissues of the head - these are sometimes called "cluster headaches"

Hormonal imbalances such as premenstrual syndrome and the peri-menopause, and side effects from the oral contraceptive pill or hormone replacement therapy

Liver dysfunction

High blood pressure

Serious causes include meningitis or brain tumours, which cause severe and unremitting headaches

Eye problems such as glaucoma or eye inflammation

Sinus, dental and ear infections

Neuralgia such as trigeminal neuralgia, which produces a sharp stabbing pain in the side of the head and face, radiating to the jaw

Blood sugar problems such as low blood sugar levels (hypoglycaemia)

Exposure to chemical toxins

Migraine headaches

Migraine is a particular type of headache characterised by severe throbbing (pulsating) pain in the whole head, or one side of the head. It may be preceded or heralded by neurological symptoms such as visual problems, weakness of the limbs or facial muscles, a spaced out weird mood, pins and needles or other frightening things. Migraine is often associated with nausea, vomiting and sensitivity to light (photophobia). The pain can be extremely severe and frightening and sometimes analgesia must be given in injection form. There are also specific medications that can be taken to prevent or abort an acute migraine, and the newest class of these drugs is known as the serotonin agonist drugs. Some find these drugs miraculous whereas others complain of side effects. Chiropractic therapy can be beneficial for many headache sufferers.

Juice for headaches

2	dandelion leaves or 2 cabbage leaves
1 cup	chopped broccoli pieces
1 cup	alfalfa sprouts
1	whole apple
1	large carrot

Wash, trim and chop and process through juicer. Drink 2 cups (approx 500ml) daily.

Options:

A few strawberries can be added to improve taste

2-3 lettuce leaves, which provides a calming effect on the nervous system.

Radish and/or garlic can be added if sinus problems are present

Wheat grass can be added if you think that body toxicity is present

Celery can be added if fluid retention and blood pressure is present

Citrus fruits to provide vitamin C, which reduces inflammation and improves circulation.

1 cm slice fresh ginger root to reduce inflammation

1 clove garlic or ½ red onion can improve circulation in migraine sufferers (migraineurs)

Useful supplements and foods -

A good liver tonic powder or capsules

Vitamin E to improve circulation

Magnesium tablets - 4 to 6 tablets daily may be required to get the headaches under control

Essential fatty acids such as cold pressed flaxseed oil and salmon oil. Consume plenty of raw salads with a dressing of cold pressed oil and apple cider vinegar.

Maintain blood sugar levels by eating regular protein from eggs, seafood, protein powder and legumes, nuts and seeds.

The intake of water must be increased to at least 2 litres daily - drink this in small amounts gradually throughout the day

HORMONAL IMBALANCES

*See Menopause - page119 , Premenstrual Syndrome - page127
and Endometriosis - page 87*

HOT FLUSHES - *see Menopause - page 120*

IMMUNE DYSFUNCTION

The immune system consists of tissues and cells that protect the body against attack from foreign invaders. It is comprised of -

White blood cells

The liver and spleen

The lymphatic system

The bone marrow

The mucous membranes in the gut and respiratory tract

The causes of immune dysfunction are -

Viral infections such as AIDS or glandular fever etc

Side effects from drugs such as - cortisone, antibiotics, immuno-suppressants or chemotherapy

Liver dysfunction

Hereditary factors

Poor dietary habits - a lack of protein and/or raw fruits and vegetables

Nutritional deficiencies of selenium, zinc and vitamin C

Immune Booster Smoothie

3	apricots (fresh or dried if not in season)
1	small ripe banana
8	almonds - grind into powder
1 tbsp	ground flaxseed
6	raisins
½ cup	coconut milk
½ cup	soy milk

Put all ingredients in blender and mix thoroughly.

Immune Booster Juice

1 stick	celery
1	ripe tomato (organic or vine-ripened are best)
1	pear
½	beetroot
1	carrot
2	dandelion leaves or cabbage leaves
1/2 cm	slice fresh ginger root
1	clove garlic (optional)
½	red onion
½	sapote or equivalent piece soursop (optional)

If soursop or sapote are unavailable, use 1" slice fresh pineapple. Sapote and soursop are nutrient dense plants.

Tomato contains lycopene, which has anti-cancer benefits

Pears are excellent for those who suffer from allergies

Beetroot is an excellent blood tonic and a good source of immune boosting nutrients

Dandelion and cabbage contain organic sulphur and support liver function

Ginger, onion and garlic have natural antibiotic properties

Carrot contains high amounts of beta-carotene, which strengthens the mucous membranes. Beta-carotene reduces the risk of many cancers.

Useful foods and supplements -

Selenium and zinc

Vitamin C and E

Essential fatty acids - flaxseed oil, evening primrose oil and oily fish

Raw nuts and seeds

Whey protein powder

Olive leaf extract is a natural antibiotic

Echinacea is an immune booster (echinacea should be avoided in those with allergies or auto-immune diseases)

Other herbs such as astragalus, andrographis or golden seal can be helpful.

INFECTIONS *- see antibiotic juice page 45*

INFLAMMATORY BOWEL DISEASE

Inflammatory Bowel Disease (IBD) includes the disorders of Ulcerative Colitis and Crohn's Disease. IBD describes the chronic inflammation that may affect the entire thickness of the bowel wall.

The symptoms of IBD may include -

Weight loss and generally poor health
Anaemia
Fevers
Nausea and vomiting
Diarrhoea - which may be bloody and/or full of mucous
Abdominal pains
Intestinal obstruction and perforation - these are surgical emergencies
There is an increased risk of bowel cancer in sufferers of IBD
There is an increased risk of liver disease in sufferers of IBD

Causes of IBD -

Hereditary factors
Poor diet high in processed foods and preserved meats, with a lack of raw fruits and vegetables
Food allergies
Unfriendly bacteria in the intestines (dysbiosis)
Overuse of antibiotics and/or chemotherapy
Immune dysfunction with a tendency to autoimmune disease

Basic Recipe for IBD

1	carrot
2	sticks celery
2	cabbage leaves or 2 dandelion leaves
4cm	slice beetroot
1	apple or 1 pear
1	spinach leaf

Options:

You may add -

2	fresh apricots or
½ cup	chopped fennel or
½	papaya or
½ cup	blackberries or
1 clove	garlic and/or ½ red onion, which exert a natural antibiotic effect in the bowel.

Warm herbal teas made from any of the following; marshmallow, golden seal, dandelion root, chamomile and/or cinnamon can be used to dilute this juice, instead of water. These herbs have a restorative effect upon the bowel.

Wash, trim and chop and pass through juicer - make enough for one litre of juice per day. You may need to dilute the juice with 50% water (or even more water), as the inflamed intestines may not be able to handle a concentrated juice. Drink small amounts (100 to 200mls) of the diluted juice, every few hours during the day, to make up a total of around one litre.

Blackberry contains phyto-nutrients, which are able to reduce intestinal inflammation.

Apple is high in pectin, which soothes the intestinal mucous membranes.

Apricot, carrot, beetroot and papaya are high in beta-carotene, which heals inflamed intestinal mucous membranes.

Dandelion and cabbage are high in organic sulphur, which heals the bowel and supports liver function.

Green leafy vegetables such as spinach are high in vitamin K, which reduces blood loss from the bowel mucosa.

All leafy vegetables and the fruits chosen in this juice are high in the minerals potassium and magnesium, which are depleted from the body in diarrhoea.

Tropical "Smoothie" to heal the bowel

1 cup	oat milk
1	ripe banana
1 tbsp	slippery elm powder
½ cup	coconut milk
2	kiwi fruit or ½ cup blackberries or 6 strawberries or ½ pawpaw. You may use less fruit if the diarrhoea is bad.

If appetite and/or digestion are poor, you may add 1 tbsp whey protein powder to this "smoothie".

Place all ingredients in a blender and blend until smooth.

Useful foods and supplements -

Acidophilus plain yogurt (if allergic to dairy use soy yogurt)

Magnesium, zinc and selenium

Oily fish and cold pressed flaxseed oil

Protein powder (whey or soy) to improve intake of protein

Grated apple

Digestive enzymes containing pancreas extract

A powder to ease the colon containing -

- Glutamine
- Glucosamine sulphate
- Slippery elm
- Fennel
- Acidophilus
- Fructo-oligosaccharides
- Pectin

Note: It is worthwhile to completely exclude dairy products and wheat for 6 months, to see if this improves food allergies and intolerances.

INSOMNIA

Poor sleep is a common problem and may consist of -

Difficulty in falling off to sleep

Light sleep with frequent awakening

Unpleasant dreams or nightmares

Early morning awakening (typically anywhere between 1am and 5am) with inability to go back to sleep

Causes of insomnia -

Depression

Stress and anxiety

Menopausal problems with a lack of oestrogen causing hot flushes

Painful conditions interfering with sleep

Noisy and/or uncomfortable sleeping environment

Bladder and/or prostate gland dysfunction resulting in the need for frequent urination during the night

Snoring and/or sleep apnoea (failure to breathe), which can be diagnosed in a Sleep Disorders Clinic

Restless legs and leg cramps

Insomnia Juice

2 to 3	large outer leaves of lettuce.
1	whole pear or 1 apple
1	carrot.
1	sweet potato (Kumara)
¼ - ½	medium bulb of fennel
1	grapefruit

Wash, trim and chop and pass through juicer. Drink half a litre daily, with half in the morning and half in the late afternoon.

Lettuce contains natural opiates, which help to relax the body

Fennel is a carminative (natural calming agent)

Vitamin C found in citrus fruits, aids breathing and oxygenation of the tissues during the night

Note: Avoid stimulants such as coffee, tea, sugar, sweet foods and alcohol during the evening, and avoid drinking excess water during the 2 hours before bed.

If hot flushes are disturbing your sleep - *see page 120*

Useful supplements -

Eat some protein before retiring to keep blood sugar levels stable during the night - some protein powder or some raw nuts or seeds, or a can of tuna will do the trick.

Magnesium tablets - 2 twice daily - I call magnesium the "great relaxer".

A herbal tea containing hops and chamomile with a tsp of honey.

A tablet containing the following combination:-
- B-group vitamins
- The herb hypericum (St Johns Wort) is helpful for depression
- Magnesium, zinc, selenium and chromium

INTESTINAL PARASITES

The intestines may harbour infections with fungi, unfriendly bacteria and parasites. These infections may be picked up from -

Unsanitary water

Food that has been contaminated with faeces from dirty hands

Travelling to far away places especially in the East.

Preserved meats (it is much safer to eat fresh well-cooked meat)

Shellfish from contaminated waters

Common infecting agents in the gut are -

Helicobacter pylori

Candida

Pathogenic (disease causing) bacteria

Giardia

Blastocystis hominus

Worms of different varieties

This juice combination will help to eradicate these infections.

Juice against intestinal parasites

2	cabbage leaves or dandelion leaves
2	spinach leaves
2	apples, whole
1	clove garlic or ½ red onion
1cm	fresh ginger root
1 cm	horse radish root
2	pomegranate (if in season) - seeds and flesh.

Wash, trim and chop all ingredients and pass through juicer. Drink 1/3 litre three times daily

You may need to dilute the juice with water.

Pomegranate is a very seasonal fruit, although its juice may be available in some health food shops. If pomegranate is unavailable, you can substitute with some of the following - parsley, cucumber, celery, carrot or beetroot.

Cabbage and dandelion are high in organic sulphur, which helps to eliminate bowel parasites.

Apple helps to improve the balance of flora (microorganisms) in the colon.

Garlic, red onion, horseradish and ginger are natural antibiotics, which help to expel parasites from the body.

Spinach reduces constipation and heals the mucous lining of the digestive tract.

Useful supplements:

Olive leaf extract and the herb Uva Ursi and grapefruit seed extract - these are all natural antibiotics.

Garlic and horseradish capsules with every meal

Avoid refined sugar, processed foods and preserved meats.

IRRITABLE BOWEL SYNDROME

Irritable Bowel Syndrome is the most common gastrointestinal disorder and raw juicing can work wonders for those who suffer with this chronic problem.

Raw Juices can save your life

Symptoms of Irritable Bowel Syndrome (IBS) are -

Abdominal bloating

Flatulence

Irregular bowel actions - there may be alternating constipation and diarrhoea

Abdominal discomfort or cramps

Causes of IBS -

Anxiety or stress

Poor dietary choices with lack of fibre and raw foods, and excessive amounts of processed and preserved foods

Food allergies

Overuse of antibiotics or steroid drugs

Juice for Irritable Bowel Syndrome

2	large apples - whole
¼	medium sized cabbage
2	sticks of celery
1	carrot
1cm	slice fresh ginger root

Wash, trim, chop and process through juicer. Drink 1 cup, 2 to 3 times a day.

Apples contain the soluble fibre pectin, which soothes the intestinal wall, reduces constipation and improves the balance of flora in the gut.

Ginger is a carminative to the digestive system and reduces flatulence.

"Smoothie" for Irritable Bowel Syndrome

1 cup	oat milk or rice milk
1	ripe banana
1 tsp	slippery elm powder
1 tsp	ground flaxseed or 1tbsp cold-pressed flaxseed oil

Place all in a blender and blend until smooth

Useful supplements and foods:

Magnesium tablets - 2 to 4 tablets daily
Slippery elm powder
FibreTone powder
Plain acidophilus yogurt
Apple cider vinegar - 1 tbsp in a glass of water (add 1 tsp honey to taste) and sip slowly during meals.
Digestive enzymes containing pancreatic enzymes

JET LAG

Jet lag is the state of mental and physical fatigue that occurs after rapid travel through different time zones. This is due to a disturbance of the brain's circadian rhythm and the endocrine glands (hormonal glands), produced by rapid changes in space and time.

Juice for Jet Lag

1	grapefruit
½	medium pineapple, peeled, cored and chopped
4	fresh mint leaves
1cm	fresh ginger root

Wash, trim and chop and pass all through the juicer. Pour over crushed ice. This juice has a stimulating effect and a rejuvenating action on the glands.

Useful supplements

Magnesium tablets
Ginseng, Guarana
Melatonin can be taken 2 to 3 hours before you want to sleep

KIDNEY DISORDERS

The kidneys filter the blood stream, removing waste products such as urea, creatinine and drugs, which are eliminated from the body via the urine. The kidneys also maintain the correct balance of minerals such as sodium and potassium in the blood. Kidney disease is common and can be silent and insidious, and may be present for years before detection. Thus it is wise to have regular urine tests and blood pressure checks.

Symptoms of kidney dysfunction and disease may include -

Back ache and/or abdominal pain

Fluid retention and swelling of the limbs

Generally poor health

Frequent and/or painful urination

Discolouration of urine

High blood pressure

Causes of kidney problems include -

Infections

Stones

Inflammation of the kidney from immune dysfunction, which is called glomerulonephritis, or nephritis for short.

Damage to the kidneys from high blood pressure

Damage to the kidneys from diabetes

Side effects from prescription drugs, or excessive use of pain killers

Dehydration

Juice for Kidney problems number one

2 to 3	sticks celery
1	carrot
½	cucumber
½	cup parsley

Optional - Plus any 2 of the following: -

½	beetroot
2	beetroot leaves
½	apple with skin on
6	strawberries
2	turnip leaves
2	dandelion leaves

Parsley, celery and cucumber are diuretics and can help to dissolve urinary tract stones.

Strawberries have mild diuretic properties and provide a delicious flavour

Turnip and dandelion support liver and kidney function and cleanse the blood stream.

Juice for kidney problems number two

10cm	slice watermelon
½	cucumber
½	peach (remove stone)
¼	cup parsley
4	string beans
1	spring onion

Watermelon and peach soothe the urinary tract.
Parsley is an excellent cleanser of the kidneys and blood stream
Cucumber has diuretic properties and reduces fluid retention
String bean juice helps to strengthen the kidneys and bladder

Useful supplements

Vitamin C (no more than 2000mg daily), in divided doses
Magnesium tablets
Olive leaf extract and garlic are excellent natural antibiotics
Herbal teas such as dandelion, nettle, Uva Ursi and golden seal

LIBIDO PROBLEMS

Libido or sex drive, can be a fragile thing and is adversely affected by many circumstances in life. Libido is also a very individual thing and what may be normal for some, may be drastically abnormal for others.

Causes of poor libido -

Stress and depression
Chronic pain
Physical pain or discomfort during sexual intercourse
Generally poor health will diminish libido
Poor diet deficient in minerals and vitamins
Excess consumption of alcohol
Hormonal deficiencies - particularly a lack of oestrogen and/or testosterone

Libido Enhancing Juice

150gm	guava fruit (also known as Fejoa) or 150gm kiwi fruit
2	passion fruit
2	oranges or 1 large grapefruit
1	raw organic egg

Wash, trim and chop the fruit (except for passionfruit), and process fruit through juicer. Put juice in blender with passionfruit pulp and egg and blend. Drink one cup twice daily.

This juice will enhance energy, sensuality and improve circulation to the vital pelvic areas.

Useful supplements -

The herbs - Ginseng, Damiana, Tribulus, Sarsaparilla, Avena sativa, Muira puama, Ginkgo biloba, and Vitamin E, C, zinc and magnesium. *The above can all be obtained, combined together in one capsule.*

Hormone replacement therapy with natural oestrogen and/or testosterone.

Boosting your libido can be very fruitful!

LIVER PROBLEMS

The liver is the largest and hardest working organ in the body. It is the filter and cleanser of the blood stream and regulates fat and carbohydrate metabolism. To put it simply, the liver is the major fat burning organ in the body, and so the state of your liver has a lot to do with your weight. A healthy liver removes toxins, dead cells and debris from the blood stream, which protects the immune system from overload. Many people who develop problems with their immune system will find that they have an underlying liver problem.

What causes liver problems -

Poor diet - high in unhealthy fats, refined carbohydrates and deficient in raw fruits and vegetables.

Infections with viruses such as hepatitis A, B and C etc.

Mineral overload from excess iron (haemochromatosis) or copper (Wilson's disease)

Side effects from prescription drugs

Alcohol and drug abuse

Immune dysfunction such as auto-immune disease

Diseases of the biliary tracts can spread to the liver

Fatty liver (infiltration of the liver with unhealthy fats)

What are the signs of liver problems -

Abdominal obesity (pot belly)

Inability to lose weight

High blood cholesterol and triglyceride levels

Fatty liver

Gall bladder problems

Haemorrhoids

Abdominal bloating

Overheating of the body

Skin problems such as rashes and brown "liver spots"

Bad breath, coated tongue, dark circles under the eyes or red itchy eyes

Immune dysfunction such as allergies and auto-immune diseases

In advanced cases jaundice (yellow colouration of the eyes and skin)

Liver Cleansing Juice

2	dandelion leaves or 2 spinach leaves or 2 large cabbage leaves
½ cup	broccoli florets
1 cup	cauliflower flowerets or 2 large Brussels sprouts
1	clove garlic or 1 small radish (optional)
½ cup	chopped parsley
1	whole red apple

Wash, trim and chop vegetables and process through juicer. This juice is high in vitamin C and sulphur compounds to cleanse the liver.

This is a very strong mixture and may be diluted 1 part juice to 1 part water or you can dilute it with cold herb or fruit flavoured tea. Drink 500 ml to 1 litre daily.

Options:
You may sweeten this juice by adding 1 or 2 of the following - strawberries, grapes, carrot or beetroot. (If you mix grapes and carrots together, it may cause flatulence)

Liver Tonic Juice.

1	carrot
125gm	fresh asparagus
125gm	cucumber - leave skin on
1	apple
2	dandelion or cabbage leaves

Wash, trim and chop all ingredients and process all in juicer. Drink 2 to 3 small cups daily.

Fatty Liver

Fatty liver is a common problem in people who are overweight, diabetic, or heavy drinkers of alcohol. The most common cause is incorrect diet, with an over consumption of fatty meats, deep fried foods, snack foods, processed foods, refined sugars and margarine. The diet is often very deficient in raw vegetables and fruits, which are needed for the liver to metabolise fats efficiently.

Fatty liver can also affect children who are obese from lack of exercise and a poor diet.

Fatty Liver Juice

2	dandelion leaves or 2 cabbage leaves
2	carrots
1	clove garlic or 5cm slice red onion
½ cup	chopped parsley
1	red radish and tops
1 cm	round slice of fennel
1/2	whole lemon
5cm	slice beetroot

Wash, trim and chop all ingredients and process through juicer. Drink 2 to 3 small cups daily.

Options:

This mixture may be very strong in flavour, and to counteract this, you may like to add some raisin juice. Soak 1 cup of raisins in enough water to cover for several hours, preferably overnight, then process fruit and liquid through juicer and add to original juice. Alternatively you can add 1 to 2 apples to the juice.

Grapefruit Bitters is another aid to fatty liver. Grind or chop the whole grapefruit - pips, pith, fruit and peel and place in a jar. Cover with water and stand with lid tightly secured overnight. Strain the liquid and drink.

For added flavour add one cup of cold lemon, ginger and honey flavoured tea, some garlic juice (optional), and top with grated nutmeg.

The above juice will stimulate the liver to burn fat, and also to pump fat out of the body through the bile into the intestines. Therefore this juice is going to be helpful for weight loss.

All the above liver juices will improve liver function and aid the repair and renewal of liver cells.

By improving liver function we are able to help many digestive problems and allergic conditions.

Another great benefit of improving the liver function is that the workload of the immune system will be reduced thus allowing the immune system to be strengthened.

Useful supplements -

A liver tonic powder, or capsules containing -

St Mary's Thistle, Globe artichoke, Dandelion, Taurine, Lecithin, Slippery elm bark and peppermint.

MENOPAUSE

Menopause is defined as the cessation of menstruation and typically occurs in women around the age of 50. It is due to the failure of the ovaries, which become totally depleted of eggs (follicles) so that the production of sex hormones ceases.

Symptoms of menopause can include -

    Hot flushes
    Poor sleep
    Aches and pains (fibromyalgia)
    Loss of sex drive
    Dryness of the vagina
    Bladder dysfunction
    Mood changes
    Fatigue

The long-term consequences of loss of the sex hormones are depletion of minerals from the bones and an increased risk of cardiovascular disease. These degenerative problems can be greatly reduced by following a healthy diet and lifestyle. In particular regular exercise becomes essential, and the diet must include unprocessed food to provide plenty of minerals such as calcium, magnesium, zinc, manganese, silica, boron and potassium.

Try to include the following in your diet -

Legumes - all types of beans, peas and lentils

Seafood and seaweeds (sea vegetables)

Raw nuts and seeds

Eggs and lean fresh meats (if not vegetarian)

Increase the amount of raw foods and raw juices in the diet

The above dietary strategies will -

Reduce osteoporosis

Reduce cardiovascular disease

Reduce your risk of cancer

Prevent excessive weight gain

Hot Flush Juice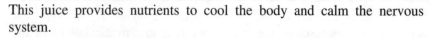

This juice provides nutrients to cool the body and calm the nervous system.

1	orange or 1 grapefruit with white pith left on
2	lettuce leaves
4cm	slice watermelon
½ cup	bean sprouts (soybean or alfalfa are most effective)
¼ cup	parsley
1	small Lebanese cucumber
3 cm	slice beetroot

Wash, trim and chop. Peel orange, leaving on as much white pith as possible. Put all ingredients through juicer.

Lettuce is cooling to the body and contains a natural sedative called lactucarium. It also contains magnesium to reduce insomnia.

Bean sprouts are high in plant hormones known as phyto-estrogens.

Watermelon is cooling and aids depression. It also contains Vitamin B to balance the nervous system.

Parsley is rich in vitamin C and bioflavonoids, which help to relieve hot flushes

Orange and grapefruit contain bioflavonoids in their white pith, which calm hot flushes.

Cucumber is cooling and calming and helps to reduce any tendency to high blood pressure, which may first arise during the menopause.

Beetroot is beneficial for energy and the blood circulation.

Menopause "Smoothie"

1 cup	calcium fortified soymilk (or if you prefer try almond, oat, coconut or rice milk)
1	banana or ½ cup berries of your choice
1 tbsp	ground flaxseed or 1tsp of cold-pressed flaxseed oil
2	passion fruit pulp

Place all ingredients into a blender and process until smooth. Add a few ice cubes while blending for a refreshing drink. Whey protein powder may be added if you need extra energy. Drink in the morning, and any time during the day.

Bananas are high in potassium, as well as vitamin B, which helps to balance the nervous system and reduce symptoms of fatigue.

Passion fruit is valuable during menopause to help with poor libido.

Flaxseeds are a superior source of healthy omega-3 fatty acids, which help to maintain hormonal balance. Omega 3 fatty acids can lower levels of the bad LDL cholesterol, which helps to protect the cardiovascular system. Flaxseed is high in lignans, which are phyto-estrogens, and reduce the risk of cancer.

Juice for Menopause number one

2	sticks celery
½	cucumber
½ cup	alfalfa sprouts
2	lettuce leaves [iceberg]
5cm	slice pineapple
3	spinach leaves

Wash, trim and chop and pass all through the juicer.

Celery contains calcium, potassium and magnesium and vitamin B, which all help to calm the nervous system.

Cucumber contains potassium and magnesium, which will help to control any blood pressure problems that may arise during menopause

Iceberg lettuce supplies calcium, potassium and magnesium as well as iron and vitamin B, which can reduce nervous tension and insomnia

Pineapple improves digestion and has a cooling effect upon the body. Spinach contains vitamin K, which is needed to maintain healthy bones and prevent osteoporosis.

Juice for Menopause number two

1	orange or 1 grapefruit (leave pith on)
2	lettuce leaves
5cm	slice watermelon
½	cup mung bean or alfalfa sprouts
¼	cup parsley
1	small Lebanese cucumber
5cm	slice beetroot

Wash, trim and chop all ingredients and pass through the juicer

Lettuce is cooling to the body and contains the natural sedative, lactucarium, as well as magnesium, which helps calm the nervous system and reduces insomnia. It also contains calcium, which helps to preserve bone density.

Mung bean and alfalfa sprouts are cooling for the liver and contain vitamin B, which calms the nervous system. Alfalfa is very high in phyto-estrogens, which reduce hot flushes and vaginal dryness.

Watermelon is cooling and aids depression.

Parsley is rich in Bioflavonoids, which help to relieve hot flushes

Orange and grapefruit contain vitamin C and bioflavonoids (especially in the white pith), which reduce hot flushes.

Cucumber is cooling and contains vitamin B, which calms the nervous system. It contains potassium, which reduces the tendency to high blood pressure.

Beetroot can be beneficial for menopausal problems, as it helps to regulate glandular problems and improves circulation.

Useful foods and supplements -

Soybeans and their products such as tofu and tempeh.

Oily fish, raw nuts and seeds.

Essential fatty acids - eg flaxseed oil and evening primrose oil.

The herbs - dong quai, black cohosh, sage, liquorice, sarsaparilla, rose hip, wild yam, kelp - these are available all combined together in some supplements for menopause.

MIGRAINE - see headaches - page 101

NERVOUS EXHAUSTION - see depression - page 77

OSTEOPOROSIS

Osteoporosis is the loss of bone mass that occurs due to the depletion of minerals from the bones. It is very common affecting 50% of women and around one third of men in their 60s. The loss of bone mineral results in weakening of the bone making it susceptible to easy breakages (fractures). There is also a loss of connective tissue in the bone, such as collagen, which makes the bones less flexible and more brittle.

Causes of osteoporosis -

Genetic factors - there is often a family history of osteoporosis

Increasing age

Lack of exercise

Smoking

Excess intake of alcohol, fizzy sweet drinks, and caffeine

Excess intake of sugar and animal protein

Thyroid problems

Drug side effects especially long term use of cortisone

Menopause and its associated hormonal deficiencies

Premature menopause (under the age of 40)

Nutritional deficiencies of minerals and anti-oxidants

Fine bone structure

Juice for Osteoporosis

4	string beans
1	carrot
2	spinach leaves
2	sprigs parsley
1	pear or 1 apple
2	Brussels sprouts
2cm	slice beetroot

Wash, trim and chop and pass all through the juicer.

The above juice provides plenty of calcium, magnesium and vitamin K, which are required for strong healthy bones.

Osteoporosis "Smoothie"

1 cup (250ml)	calcium fortified soy or coconut milk
4	dried apples
8	dried apricots
30g	unblanched almonds

Soak apples and apricots in hot water for one hour. Drain fruit and cool. Place drained fruit, the draining water, and all the other ingredients in a blender and blend until smooth

Almonds are high in calcium. Dried fruit contains the mineral boron, which is needed for bone building and healthy calcium metabolism.

Useful supplements to build bone density -
A Bone and Joint Nutrients capsule containing a combination of -

- Calcium hydroxyapatite
- Zinc
- Silica
- Selenium
- Glucosamine

- Magnesium
- Copper
- Horsetail
- Vitamin D
- Manganese

PAIN RELIEF

Pain Relief Juice

This juice contains anti-oxidants and anti-inflammatory ingredients. It also contains substances to build and repair the nervous system.

125g	chopped broccoli
1 cm	slice fresh ginger root
2	oranges or 1 grapefruit - leave white pith on
3	strawberries
1 tsp	fresh wheat germ oil
1 tsp	fresh lecithin granules
1 tsp	ground flaxseed or 1 tsp of flaxseed oil

Wash, trim and chop broccoli, ginger and orange/grapefruit and pass through the juicer. Pour the juice into a blender and add strawberries, wheat germ, lecithin and flaxseed. Blend until smooth. If you are brave, you can add a small chilli pepper (or a small part thereof) to the juicer, as its contained capsaicin increases the release of the brain's endorphins. Endorphins are natural painkillers.

PERIODONTAL DISEASE

Periodontal disease is the term for inflammation and chronic infection of the gums. This causes the gums to shrink so that a receding gum line develops, which makes the teeth appear longer. The roots of the teeth may become exposed causing unpleasant sensitivity of the gums and teeth, especially to hot and cold temperatures or to touch. Eventually there is considerable loss of gum tissue, which results in loosening of the teeth. Periodontal disease is the most common cause of teeth loss. Periodontal disease is often associated with bone loss in the jaws and also in other parts of the skeleton (osteoporosis).

Causes

Plaque formation on the teeth.
Poor cleaning of the teeth - it is vital to floss, use toothpicks, or interdental brushes every day.
Lack of minerals in the diet - especially if the diet consists of processed and refined foods.

Eating excess amounts of sugary foods and cola drinks.

Lack of raw fruits and vegetables in the diet.

Smoking and alcohol excess.

It is more common at the time of menopause, so hormonal changes may be significant.

Juice for the Gums and Teeth

2 to 3	dandelion leaves or spinach leaves
1-cup	parsley leaves
1cm	fresh ginger root
1	whole apple
1	whole orange or grapefruit
1	carrot

Wash, trim and chop and process through juicer. Drink approximately ½ litre daily.

Useful supplements -

Calcium hydroxyapatite, Magnesium, Selenium and Zinc, Silica, Cod liver oil or vitamin D, Vitamin C, Olive leaf extract capsules

PREGNANCY

During pregnancy there is an increased need for folic acid, iron, calcium and essential fatty acids. By increasing your intake of folic acid (folate) you are able to reduce the risk of neural tube defects such as Spina Bifida by 70%. Neural tube defects are common congenital abnormalities in newborn babies, and cause severe defects in the spinal cord and sometimes the brain.

Juice for Pregnancy

2	spinach leaves
½	cup chopped broccoli
2	Brussels sprouts or 1 carrot
1	orange
1	beetroot and tops
1	tomato (vine ripened or organic is best)

Wash, trim and chop ingredients and pass all through the juicer. Dilute with water or cold chamomile tea, especially if morning sickness or nausea is problematic. The addition of a whole pear and/or apple can improve the flavour of this juice.

This juice provides extra folate (folic acid), vitamin K, iron and calcium. It also helps to support liver and kidney function, which will reduce the risk of toxaemia of pregnancy. Women who obtain plentiful antioxidants and vitamin K during pregnancy, will have a reduced risk of abnormal bleeding from the placenta and therefore premature labour.

Useful supplements for pregnancy -

Calcium and iron
Folic acid
Essential fatty acids from flaxseed oil, evening primrose oil and oily fish
Homoeopathic "ipecac" or "nux vomica" for nausea
Injections of vitamin B 6 and B 12 can reduce nausea & vomiting of pregnancy

PREMENSTRUAL SYNDROME

Premenstrual Syndrome (PMS) is a collection of symptoms that occurs during the last 2 weeks of the menstrual cycle. Typical symptoms of PMS are -

Mood changes such as depression and anxiety
Personality changes
Extreme irritability
Fatigue
Pelvic discomfort
Headaches
Acne and pimples
Weight gain

Cause of PMS

The cause is hormonal imbalance characterised by a relative deficiency of the two female hormones (oestrogen and progesterone) during the one to two weeks before menstrual bleeding occurs.

This hormonal imbalance may be triggered by -

Poor diet and lifestyle

Tubal ligation

Post-natal depression

Getting older and arriving at the pre-menopause

Juice for PMS

2 to 3	spinach leaves or dandelion leaves
2	lettuce leaves
1	orange (leave white pith on)
1	medium beetroot & tops
½ cup	chopped parsley or ½ cucumber

Wash, trim and chop and process through juicer. Drink approximately ½ litre daily.

Options:

Add a generous slice of fresh pineapple to the juice to assist in regulating the menstrual cycle.

Add blackberries to the juice, as they are a good general tonic and have a calming effect on menstrual cramping.

Useful supplements and hormones -

Some women with persistent PMS will need to use natural progesterone in the form of lozenges or creams during the last 2 weeks of the menstrual cycle. When the menstrual bleeding commences, stop the progesterone until the next PMS cycle begins.

Cold pressed flaxseed oil.

Minerals - calcium, magnesium, zinc and iron.

Vitamin B complex.

Female herbs such as dong quai and liquorice, black cohosh, chamomile etc.

There are women's formulas available, which combine all these nutrients/herbs in one tablet.

REJUVENATING JUICE RECIPES

Perhaps you are not really sick and have no real problems you can look up in this book. That's great news! However it's not wise to rest on your laurels!

Your cells need a continual supply of living nutrients to provide you with the energy and immune resistance you need to get through your day.

Why not add to your savings account of health with a smorgasbord of nutrients from a variety of the following delicious juices?

There are many combinations of juices, which will give you a boost to start the day and leave you feeling invigorated with enough energy to cope with a busy demanding schedule.

Choose the Juice of any 2 Fruits in Season

OR

Try some of the following interesting combinations-

Equal portions of carrot and apple, plus ½cm of fresh ginger root.

Equal portions of carrot, celery, tomato and apple, plus ½ cup chopped parsley and 4-6 mint leaves.

Equal portions of beetroot, apple and pear, plus 1 cm of fresh ginger root, plus ½ cup chopped parsley.

One whole orange and lemon, 1 large carrot or 1 cm fresh ginger root, plus 1 cup of chopped parsley.

Equal quantities of prune juice and grapefruit juice, plus 1 tsp of honey.

One pear, 1 red apple, 1 medium lemon, 1 tsp honey and a sprinkle of cinnamon.

4 fresh apricots (remove stones), 1 small lemon and ½ tsp honey.

4 plums (remove stones), 1 small orange, a pinch of nutmeg and 2 mint leaves.

Chapter 4

SINUS (also hay fever)

Sinus problems are common and typically cause pain in the forehead and the cheek bone and nasal area. Nasal congestion and discharge is common so that difficulty breathing through the nose is experienced. Attacks of sneezing and watery nasal discharge may occur, and the eyes may be red and itchy.

Causes of sinus and hay fever

Infection with bacteria and viruses

Allergy to airborne pollens, pollution and foods. The most common food intolerances are to dairy products, wheat, and food additives.

Swelling of the lymphatic tissue above and behind the nasal passages.

Juice for Sinus

1	small red radish
1 cm	fresh ginger root
1	clove garlic, <u>or</u> ½ small red onion <u>or</u> 1cm slice horseradish
¼	of a fresh pineapple
1	carrot or 2 fresh apricots (if in season)
1	orange or half a grapefruit (leave white pith on)

The first 3 ingredients all have a strong flavour, so don't overdo the quantities until your palate can cope with the flavour.

Wash, trim, peel and chop and process through juicer.

Drink half a litre at any time during the day.

This juice can be diluted with water, or warm lemon and ginger tea.

Radish, garlic, onions and fresh ginger have natural antibiotic properties to help reduce infections and also eliminate mucous from the nasal passages.

Carrot and apricots contain beta-carotene, which helps to heal and promote healthy mucous membranes.

Pineapple has anti-inflammatory properties and contains natural enzymes, which help to break up tenacious mucous.

Useful supplements -

Garlic and horseradish tablets

Vitamin C and bioflavonoids

Selenium and zinc can reduce the incidence of infections

Olive leaf extract capsules or elixir are excellent if infection is present

Steam inhalations can be done with 2 drops of tea tree oil added to the hot water

Avoid all dairy products and food additives

Spicy food such as wasabi paste, curry, mustard, and chilli help to clear the nasal passages

SKIN

The appearance of your skin reflects your inner health. The skin helps to regulate your body temperature by dispersing heat through perspiration. It also plays a large role in the elimination of body toxins and wastes. The skin utilises sunshine to synthesise Vitamin D, which is essential for the immune system and bones.

The skin has been called a 'third kidney'. This is because its appearance reflects the build up of wastes in the body that occurs when there is an overload of the other excretory channels such as the liver, bowels and kidneys. If we improve the function of these excretory organs, the appearance of the skin will improve.

The most common skin problems are -

Eczema (also known as dermatitis)

Psoriasis

Brown blemishes (also known as liver spots)

Skin cancer

Wrinkling and ageing of the skin

Dryness of the skin

Itchy skin (also known as pruritus)

Skin infections with viruses, fungal and bacterial organisms.

Acne

Vitiligo - depigmentation of the skin

Chapter 4

Common causes of skin problems -

Genetic factors (a family history of eczema and psoriasis is common)
Stress and anxiety
Underlying problems with the immune system
Liver dysfunction
Overexposure to the sun and/or harsh chemicals or soaps
Contact with irritants or allergens (contact dermatitis)
Hormonal imbalances
Nutritional deficiencies

Possible Combinations of Juices for Healthy Skin

The following table contains juices that are beneficial for the healing and conditioning of your skin. You may choose to drink the juice of any of the ingredients either singularly, when in season, or any number of them together, to suit your own taste.

Why not create your own delicious combinations.

An ideal mixture is 1 to 2 of the greens, with 3 to 4 of the other ingredients.

Greens	Others	Others
Cucumber	Grapes	Plums
Lettuce	Apple	Strawberries
Cabbage	Apricots	Mango
Watercress	Pear	Orange
Dandelion leaf	Carrot	Tomato

* Choose ripe unblemished fruits and vegetables.

* If you experience flatulence, dilute the juices with water, or reduce the number of combinations in one juice.

* You need to drink at least 500mls (half a litre) daily to show good results.

Skin juice

1	carrot
½	beetroot & tops
2	sticks celery and tops
½	cucumber
2	spinach or dandelion leaves
1	grapefruit or orange (retain as much white pith as possible)

Wash, trim and chop and process in juicer.
Can dilute with water or cold lemon and honey tea

Some popular juices to enhance skin health and beauty are: -

Strawberry Treat

500g	fresh strawberries (organic is preferable)
1	orange
3	fresh mint leaves

You may add a teaspoon of honey if desired. Honey is anti-microbial and helps to liven up the 'spritzy' taste of this delicious drink

Wash, trim and chop and process through juicer. Pour into a glass with a few ice cubes and some whole fresh strawberries.

Tomato Cocktail

Equal quantities of fresh apple and tomato, juiced with 2 - 3 leaves of fresh basil.

Fresh tomato juice contains Vitamin C and cleanses the liver, which is then reflected in clearer glowing skin.

Apple juice helps assimilation, and increases utilisation of the nutrients in the other juice ingredients.

Basil aids digestion and has a cleansing action on the skin.

Raisin Cocktail

½ cup	raisins soaked overnight in pure water - enough to cover the fruit
1	orange or 1 small grapefruit
½ cup	fresh grapes
1	whole pear
1	medium carrot
A pinch	of ground nutmeg.

Prepare raisins and soak overnight. Wash, trim and chop other ingredients and process in juicer. Put juice into blender with raisins and the water in which they have been soaked. Blend until smooth and pour into glass and sprinkle with nutmeg.

Useful supplements and foods

Essential fatty acids are vital for dry, itchy and inflamed skin - best sources are cold pressed flaxseed oil, evening primrose oil, borage oil and oily fish such as sardines, salmon and tuna. Raw nuts and seeds are also good sources of essential fatty acids.

Selenium and zinc are vital for healthy skin, and are able to reduce skin infections and the formation of skin cancers.

Organic sulphur in the form of MSM powder. Sulphur is also found in the cruciferous vegetables such as cauliflower, cabbage, Brussels sprouts and broccoli and vegetables of the onion family (garlic, onions, leeks and shallots). Sulphur has a cleansing and healing effect on the skin.

These supplements and foods are vitally important and need to be taken regularly.

STOMACH ULCER

(This also applies to other ulcers of the digestive tract)

Ulcers of the stomach and duodenum are known as peptic ulcers. It used to be thought that all peptic ulcers were due to excessive acid production from the stomach lining (*mucosa*).

It is now known that a bacteria, called Helicobacter Pylori, which lives in the *mucosa* of the stomach, is the cause of many peptic ulcers.

Other contributing factors towards peptic ulcers are -

Excess intake of analgesics and anti-inflammatory drugs

Smoking and alcohol abuse

Stress and anxiety

A diet high in sugary foods, which feeds the Helicobacter Pylori bacteria

Nutritional deficiencies

Changes in gut secretions are affected by our emotions. Ulcers can stem from lifelong patterns of emotional response such as resentment, anger and frustration. It is important to be able to channel emotions such as anger into more productive ways of dealing with any of life's problems.

Peptic Ulcer Juice

2 to 3	large cabbage leaves
1-cup	alfalfa sprouts
1	carrot
2	sticks celery
1	red apple (skin on)
½ cup	aloe vera juice - [available at health food shops], or juice some fresh leaves.

Wash, trim and chop and process through juicer. This juice can then be put into a blender with the aloe vera juice for more through mixing.

Options:

You may need to dilute this juice by 1 part juice/2 parts water, or add a little more carrot and apple juice.

Drink at least 500 ml to 1 litre of this juice, in 3 to 4 divided doses during the day.

> Cabbage cleanses and breaks up waste matter in the intestines and stomach. Cabbage is specific for inflammation and/or ulceration of the stomach and indeed the entire digestive tract.

> Apple contains pectin, which improves the balance of gut flora and is soothing to the intestines.

> Aloe Vera contains long chain sugars, one of which is called Acemannan. It acts as an anti-inflammatory agent and neutralizes many of the toxins that are responsible for damaging the mucosal wall. It is bactericidal as well as fungicidal and helps to protect the gastrointestinal lining.

"Smoothie" for Peptic Ulcers

2 cups	oat milk
1	ripe banana
1 tbsp	whey protein concentrate powder
1 tbsp	slippery elm powder
1 tbsp	cold pressed flaxseed oil

Place all ingredients in a blender and blend until smooth. Serve "smoothie" with 3 organic strawberries or 1/3 cup fresh berries on the side.

THYROID DYSFUNCTION AND/OR GOITRE

Thyroid problems are very common especially in women around the time of the menopause. The most common type of thyroid problem is underactivity of the gland, which is called hypothyroidism. In this disorder the thyroid gland is not able to manufacture sufficient amounts of thyroid hormone. Thyroid hormone controls the metabolic rate of the body speeding up the rate at which the cells convert food energy into physical energy. Goitre is the term used to describe enlargement of the thyroid gland, which is most commonly caused by multiple cysts forming within the gland.

Symptoms of an under-active thyroid gland -

Weight gain
Low body temperature
Constipation
Hair loss
Dry flaky skin
Fluid retention
Slow reflexes
Fatigue
Rapid ageing
Slowness of thought and cognition

Causes of thyroid disease -

Endemic deficiency of minerals such as iodine and selenium
Auto-immune disease - known as Hashimoto's thyroiditis
Viral infection of the thyroid gland
Genetic factors - there is often a family history of thyroid diseases
Cancer of the thyroid gland

Juice for the Thyroid Gland

1 cm	fresh ginger root
1	red radish & leaf
2	carrots
1	medium beetroot and tops
2 to 3	lettuce leaves
1 tsp	kelp powder

Wash, trim and chop and process through juicer all vegetables and leaves. Then stir the kelp powder through the juice.

Options:

You may add a 4cm slice of fresh pineapple, or 2 spinach leaves and a medium sized tomato to enhance the flavour.

If you find the juice too strong for your taste, dilute with 50% water.

Drink ½ litre of this juice during the day.

Radish and carrot are good sources of iodine, which stimulates thyroid function. Iodine is essential for the production of thyroid hormone.

Beetroot contains vitamin B6 and minerals, which are needed in the manufacture of thyroid hormone.

Helpful supplements -

Kelp and other seaweeds (*such as arame, wakame, nori etc.*), are an excellent source of iodine and other trace minerals to support thyroid function.

Sea salt is high in minerals.

Selenium, which is needed for the conversion of thyroid hormone into its active form in the body.

Essential fatty acids such as cold pressed flaxseed oil.

ULCERATIVE COLITIS - *see Inflammatory Bowel Disease (IBD) page 105*

VARICOSE VEINS (this also applies to blood clots and deep vein thrombosis)

Varicose veins are enlarged swollen veins, which appear most commonly on the legs and feet. Haemorrhoids are varicose veins of the lower bowel (rectum). The veins are swollen because their walls become weakened and thin. This is due to degeneration of the connective tissues in the vein walls and increased pressure inside the veins.

Many people with varicose veins have surgery to strip the swollen veins, however the varicose veins often recur, if nutritional medicine is not used to treat the cause.

The causes of varicose veins are -

Sluggish blood flow in the veins due to poor muscle tone in the legs

Lack of exercise

Nutritional deficiencies of antioxidants and minerals required to keep the vein walls strong

Congestion of the liver

Constipation

Pregnancy which increases the pressure inside the veins

Hereditary factors and there is often a family history of varicose veins

Obesity which increases the pressure within the veins

Blood clots and blockages within the deep veins of the legs

Hormonal changes such as high levels of female hormones during pregnancy or from the oral contraceptive pill or potent hormone replacement therapy

Deep vein thrombosis is more common in those with varicose veins.

Raw Juices can save your life

Juice for Varicose Veins and Blood Clots

125g	blue berries or blackberries
125g	raspberries
1cm	fresh ginger root
½	clove garlic or ¼ red onion
1	grapefruit - leave white pith on

Wash, trim and chop the ingredients. Pass the gingerroot, garlic, onion and grapefruit through the juicer. Add this juice to a blender with the berries and blend until smooth.

The above juice will strengthen the vein walls and thin the blood. It will reduce the risk of blood clots forming in the blood vessels. Berries contain bioflavonoids, which strengthen the vein walls and reduce inflammation in the veins. Ginger, garlic and onions thin the blood and improve blood flow. Grapefruit provides vitamin C and bioflavonoids to improve circulation and strengthen blood vessel walls.

WEIGHT EXCESS - *See also "Body Shaping"- page 53*

It will be a relief to many to know that raw juicing can help with weight loss. I had a female patient who told me that she managed to lose quite a lot of weight simply by increasing the raw food component of her diet and using raw juices. She did not change her diet in any other way and found it surprising to see the kilograms coming off!

More than half of adult Australians are overweight and nearly 20% are obese. There are approximately 7 million Australians battling with their weight.

Raw juicing improves the circulation to the fat cells, which reduces cellulite. The juices also stimulate the ability of the liver to burn fat.

**For more information on nutrients for Your Body Type,
Phone a Body Shaping counsellor on 02 4655 8855**

To discover your Body Type NOW visit
www.weightcontroldoctor.com and do the interactive
questionnaire on line.

Weight Loss Juice Number One

This juice will promote weight loss and reduce the occurrence of cellulite. It is also a great liver cleanser.

1	large whole grapefruit - pink if available
2	dandelion leaves
1	medium whole apple
½ cup	chopped parsley
1	medium carrot
1	medium cucumber - Lebanese is ideal
1	pinch or ¼ tsp turmeric
½ tsp	Kelp powder

Wash, trim and chop all fruit, vegetables and leaves, and process through juicer. Then add turmeric and kelp powder. This juice can be diluted 1 part juice to 1 part water or cold lemon & honey tea.

Grapefruit is traditionally known for it's weight reducing properties.
Dandelion, Cucumber and Parsley have natural diuretic properties.
Turmeric is an effective liver tonic.
Kelp stimulates the function of the thyroid gland.

Weight Loss Juice Number Two

A mixture of equal quantities of spinach and beetroot with tops

or

any of the following would be useful-
> Carrot & Spinach
> Carrot & Lettuce
> Cabbage & Tomato
> Pineapple & Grapefruit

Any of these juices may also be diluted 1 part juice - 1 part water

Options:

To enhance these flavours you may add one quarter cup of any of the following juices :

- Celery, cucumber, orange, lemon, grapefruit, strawberry, apricot, peach, pear or pomegranate.

The Lean Green Mama says...

"A juice a day keeps the doctor away!"

Chapter 5

Juices and Smoothies
Purely for Healthy Enjoyment
(for Children and Adults)

Coconut & Apricot Smoothie

250g	fresh apricots
1-cup	coconut milk (fresh or tinned)
4-6	Strawberries or raspberries or blackberries if desired

Remove stones from apricots, wash and process through juicer and place in a blender with coconut milk and berries. Serve with a pinch of ground nutmeg and ice.

Orange, Mango and Apricot Delight

125g	apricots
1	large orange, peeled but leave plenty of pith
150g	mango fruit - peeled

Wash fruit, remove stones, chop and process through juicer. This juice is high in Vitamin C and beta-carotene, and is excellent for skin problems.

Tropical Delight (Something like a non-alcoholic pina colada)

1-cup	coconut milk - fresh or canned
¼	fresh pineapple
4 - 6	strawberries, blackberries or raspberries

Wash, trim and process the pineapple through juicer. Add the pineapple juice to berries and coconut milk and blend in a blender. Serve over crushed ice.

Yummy Healthy "Smoothie"

1 cup	soy milk (or oat, rice or almond milk)
1	ripe banana
1 tsp	ground flaxseed or cold-pressed flaxseed oil
1 tsp	fresh wheat germ
4 - 6	strawberries or other fresh berries

One raw organic egg may be added if you are trying to put on weight, or if you need to increase your protein intake. The egg must be fresh and refrigerated, as eggs can carry the salmonella bacteria.

Put all ingredients into a blender and blend until silky smooth. This is a great smoothie for building the immune system and is helpful for digestive disorders.

Best enjoyed by adding crushed ice.

Berry Delicious

125g	strawberries
125g	raspberries
125g	blueberries

Wash all fruit thoroughly and process through juicer.

Apricot & Banana Cocktail

250g	fresh apricots (can use dried apricots if fresh unavailable)
250g	ripe banana
2/3 cup	coconut milk - (canned is fine)
1 tsp	freshly squeezed lemon juice

Stand apricots in water overnight (both fresh or dried). Remove stones and chop and process in juicer with lemon juice. If using dried apricots place them in blender after soaking.

In a blender - blend banana and coconut milk, then add apricot juice (or soaked dried apricots) and blend until smooth. Delicious served with crushed ice and a sprinkle of cinnamon.

Grape Nectar

2	bunches grapes [white or dark]
2	lemons - juiced
500ml	water
1 - 2 tsp	honey to taste.

Wash grapes, process in juicer, add lemon juice, water and honey. Serve over ice with a slice of lemon.

Orange Energiser

500 ml	fresh orange juice
2 tbsp	fresh lemon juice
250ml	water or cold orange or lemon tea
6 - 8	strawberries or other berries (halved)

Honey to taste.

Mix juices and honey together and toss in halved berries - Serve.

Raisin Juice Cocktail

1-cup raisins, soaked in hot water overnight
1-cup fresh grapes
1   orange - peeled

Process all fruit in juice extractor. Stir in the water in which raisins were soaked. This juice is a great vitality booster and all round "feel good drink".

Good Morning Juice

1-cup prunes, soaked overnight in 1 cup of hot water
Equal amounts of grapefruit juice, approx 1 - 2 grapefruit.

Remove stones from prunes and process with water in a blender. Add squeezed grapefruit juice and a little honey if desired.

Pineapple Pick-Me-Up

½   fresh pineapple
1   medium grapefruit peeled
1   medium apple - skin on
1cm   slice of fresh ginger root, or pinch of ground ginger
1 tsp honey

Wash, trim and chop and process all in a juicer. Last of all, stir in the honey.

Serve over crushed ice.

Peachy Pleaser

2   large peaches (nectarines can also be used) - fruit must be ripe and unblemished
1   lemon - juiced
1 tsp honey

Remove stones from fruit; rub peach skin gently until smooth, process through juicer. Add lemon juice and honey.

Tomato Refresher

Process in a blender equal quantities of fresh tomatoes (organic or vine-ripened is best) and apple juice, together with 2 - 3 fresh basil leaves and 4 fresh mint leaves. When serving, add about 1 tsp of honey to taste.

For those who like it spicy, add a few drops of Tabasco sauce (chilli)

Watermelon Refresher

1-cup	Watermelon Juice
2 stems	celery
4 - 6	mint leaves (pineapple sage is also tasty)

Peel watermelon leaving a little pith, chop celery and mint or sage leaves, and process all in juicer. Delicious served with crushed ice.

Spiced Watermelon Cocktail

Enough watermelon to make 1-cup juice

1	medium apple - skin on
½	Lebanese cucumber
¼ cup	lemon juice

Pinch to ¼ tsp allspice

Chop fruit, cucumber, and process in juicer. Stir in lemon juice and allspice.

Serve chilled or over ice.

Melons with Melons

375g	watermelon
375g	cantaloupe
375g	honeydew melon

1cm slice of fresh ginger root, or ¼ tsp ground ginger

2 - 4 mint leaves

Peel and chop melons and process all ingredients in juicer. This juice can be diluted with 2 parts juice to 1 part water if desired. Also delicious with 1 dessertspoon natural soy yogurt, whipped into juice.

Pear and Apple Energiser "Smoothie"

1	ripe pear
1	apple
1-cup	soy milk (or rice, oat, coconut or almond milk)
1 tsp	honey
1 tsp	LSA (Linseed, Sunflower seed, Almond) - available at health food stores
1 tsp	fresh lecithin granules
1 dsp	natural soy yoghurt.

Use ripe, unblemished fruit. Wash and chop ingredients. Place all ingredients in blender and process until smooth. Chill or serve over crushed ice with a sprinkle of cinnamon.

Banana/Passion fruit Cocktail

1-cup	soy milk (or rice, oat, coconut or almond milk)
1	banana - ripe
1 tsp	honey
1 tsp	ground flaxseed or cold-pressed flaxseed oil
1 dsp	ground almonds
1	passion fruit (pulp)
1 tbsp	desiccated coconut

Place all ingredients in blender and blend until smooth. Yum!!!

Good Morning Starter

1-cup	soy milk (or rice, oat, coconut or almond milk)
1 cup	fresh chopped stone fruit (in season)
1	small ripe banana
1 tbsp	cold pressed flaxseed oil
1 tbsp	LSA (Linseed, Sunflower seeds and Almonds, ground together in a grinder or food processor)
1 tbsp	soybean or Vitari ice-cream, or 1 dsp of honey

Remove stone from fruit - (use ripe unblemished fruit) and place all ingredients in blender and blend until smooth. This drink can be taken as a snack, or as a meal replacement, and you can add a fresh egg or whey protein powder for extra nourishment and protein. Sprinkle with cinnamon and serve immediately.

Your Choice

These recipes will have given you lots of ideas, so now try a mixture of your own ingredients, either in a juice extractor or blender.

If using a milk base - avoid dairy and use soy, rice, oat, almond or coconut milk. This will help lessen mucous production in the body. [Some people who have allergies, cannot handle soy, so substitute any of the above-mentioned milks]

If you eat yoghurt - use soy or low-fat plain dairy yoghurt

If you like ice cream - use soy, Vitari or any non-dairy ice-cream [preferably not containing added sugar].

Your choices are limited only by your imagination.

**Put your thinking cap on and drink
- to health and longevity!**

Glossary

ANTIBIOTIC
Substances which fight infection.

BETA-CAROTENE
The precursor that the body needs to manufacture Vitamin A. Also known as pro-vitamin A.

BIOFLAVONOIDS
Are found with vitamin C in plants. Bioflavonoids help strengthen the walls of blood vessels and reduce inflammation.

CANDIDA
Is a yeast that exists widely in nature. It often exists in the body without causing any problems. Candida can cause opportunistic infections in the gut, skin and vagina if the immune system is weakened, or after antibiotic treatment.

CHLOROPHYLL
Is the pigment found in green plants. Chlorophyll is cleansing and builds the haemoglobin levels of the blood, as well as providing excellent nutrition for ailing cells.

ENDOCRINE SYSTEM
Consists of the glands that manufacture and secrete hormones.

ESSENTIAL FATTY ACIDS
These are necessary to maintain healthy cells. They are not made by the body but are sourced from foods such as fish, fish oil, seeds & nuts and their oils, as well as evening primrose oil.

FIBROMYALGIA
An inflammatory disorder causing symptoms of muscle and joint pain, tenderness and stiffness.

GUT FLORA - The type and balance of living micro-organisms found within the intestines.

HAEMOGLOBIN
Is a protein- iron complex molecule found within red blood cells, which transports oxygen around the body.

Raw Juices can save your life

HELICO-BACTER
A bacteria that invades the wall of the stomach and duodenum and is a causative factor in ulcerous conditions.

MACULAR DEGENERATION
Degeneration of the macula, which is the part of the retina, [at the back of the eye], that is responsible for fine vision

OMEGA OILS
Are fatty acids divided into the series, omega-3 and omega-6, which are present in some vegetables, nuts, seeds, legumes, grains and seafood. Essential fatty acids form the major structural parts of the cell walls and are needed to make prostaglandins.

OSTEOPOROSIS
When bone mass is lost due to depletion of minerals. The bones become brittle and porous.

OXALIC ACID
Is contained in some vegetables and protein containing foods. Excessive amounts of spinach, rhubarb, tea, coffee or chocolate, can promote the formation of oxalic acid stones in the urinary system.

PRO-ANTHOCYANIDINS
Are flavonoids responsible for the red-blue colour of berries. They stabilise the protein structures in the body and act as antioxidants.

PROSTAGLANDINS
Natural chemicals, which the body manufactures. They act like hormone messengers and control inflammation and circulation.

SYNDROME - X
A chemical imbalance which makes you store FAT!

TOXAEMIA
Poisoning of the body, often from internal chemical reactions, infections, leaky gut and liver problems.

References

Blauer, S., The Juicing Book, 1989, Avery Publishing, NY

Cabot, Dr. S., The Body Shaping Diet, 1993, Women's Health Advisory Service, Australia

Clinkard, C.E., The Uses of Juices, 1997, Penguin Books, N.Z.

Davies, Dr. S & Stewart, Dr A., Nutritional Medicine, 1987, Cox & Wyman, Berkshire,

Jacka, J., A-Z of Natural Therapies, 1987, Lothian Publishing, Australia

Kadans, J.M., Encyclopedia of Medicinal Herbs, 1970, Parker Publishing, NY

Kadans, J.M., Encyclopedia of Medicinal Foods, 1973, Parker Publishing, NY

Murray, M & Pizzorno, J., Encyclopaedia of Natural Medicine, 1990, Macdonald & Co., London

Osiecki, H., The Nutrient Bible, 1998, Bio Concepts Publishing, Australia

Pedersen, Nutritional Herbology, 1987, Pedersen Publishing, Utah

Schauenberg P, Guide to Medicinal Plants,1997, Lutterworth Press, Great Britain

Smith, Dr. L., Feed Yourself Right, 1983, Doubleday, Australia

Tenney, L. Today's Herbal Health, 1983, Woodland Books, Australia

Walker, N.W., Fresh Vegetable and Fruit Juices, 1978, Norwalk Press, AZ

Wood, R, The Whole Foods Encyclopedia, 1988, Prentice Hall, New York

Raw Juices can save your life

My Favourite Recipes

Notes

My Favourite Recipes

DR SANDRA CABOT HEALTH FORMULAS

MSM Plus Vitamin C Powder
MSM is Methyl Sulphonyl Methane and is organic natural sulphur. This is a valuable aid for –
Liver function
Arthritis and fibromyalgia
Hair loss and skin problems

Glicemic Balance
Glicemic Balance contains natural substances to help blood sugar stabilization. It is helpful for –
Syndrome X – the chemical imbalance that makes you store fat
Cravings for carbohydrates and sugary foods

Metabocel
Metabocel is a weight loss formula containing Brindle berry and synergistic factors. It is helpful for –
Fat burning
To stimulate a sluggish metabolism in men and women

Body Type Supplements
There are 4 different Body Types and each has unique hormonal and metabolic characteristics. To discover your Body Type do our interactive questionnaire at www.weightcontroldoctor.com
Dr Cabot's Body Type supplements balance your hormones and metabolism for your Body Type to enable weight loss to occur from where you need to lose weight.

Olive leaf tablets and Elixir
This acts as a natural antibiotic to fight infections.

"Livatone" and "Livatone Plus" liver tonics
These special formulas are available in capsule and powder form, and are designed to be the liver tonics for Today's World
Love your liver and Live Longer!

FibreTone powder – natural vanilla flavour
A natural fibre product which aids sluggish and toxic bowels. FibreTone is a Superfood for the bowels and is free of gluten and psyllium. FibreTone is helpful for Irritable Bowel Syndrome and Constipation.

Raw Juices can save your life

FemmePhase

Natural formula for Menopause to balance the hormones and improve libido. Contains natural plant estrogens and calcium plus vitamins and minerals.

Magnesium Complete tablets

This tablet contains 5 different types of magnesium for better absorption and efficacy. Helpful for –

Headaches and migraines

Arthritis and cramps

Stress and anxiety

Magnesium Complete – **The Great Relaxer!**

Selenomune Powder

This is an energy powder to help the immune system and reduce inflammation. Selenomune powder is helpful for the thyroid gland and inflammatory problems.

Hormone Creams

Sensual Passion Cream containing androstenedione and MSM.

Natural Progesterone and MSM cream

Thyroid Cream to boost metabolism

(These statements have not been evaluated by the FDA. These suggestions are not intended to diagnose, treat or cure any diseases.

Dr Sandra Cabot's Health Books

Menopause – HRT and it's Natural Alternatives

The Body Shaping Diet Book

The Liver Cleansing Diet Book

The Healthy Liver & Bowel Book

Boost Your Energy Book

Can't lose weight? You could have Syndrome X! - This is the ONLY book that looks at all the hidden and medical reasons that stop you from losing weight

Dr Sandra Cabot's Free Magazine

Is a full colour glossy Magazine on weight control and hormonal imbalances

To obtain your FREE copy phone 623 334 3232 or 180075LIVER

COLOUR IN

Lean Green Mama

An apple a day keeps the doctor away!

Raw Juices can save your life

SPOT 10 DIFFERENCES & COLOUR IN

ANSWERS: 1.Carrot's tongue, 2.Beetroot, 3.Juice machine switch, 4.Strawberry's eye, 5.Pouring juice, 6.'O' in 'of', 7.'I' in 'life', 8.Pear's eyebrow, 9.Tomato's hair, 10.Celery's chin.

CONVERSION TABLE

WEIGHTS		LIQUIDS		
Ounces (oz)	Grams (g)	Fluid Ounces (oz)	Millilitres (ml)	cups/tbsp
1	30	1	30	2tbsp
2	60	2	60	4tbsp
3	90	3	80	1/3 cup
4	125	4	125	½ cup
5	155	5	160	2/3 cup
6	185	6	180	¾ cup
7	220	8	250	1 cup
8	250	10	310	1&1/4 cup
10	315	12	375	1 & ½ cup
12	375	14	430	1 & ¾ cup
14	440	16	500	2 cups
16 (1 pound)	500	24	750	3 cups
1.5 pounds	750	32	1000 (1 litre)	4 cups
2 pounds	1000 (1 kg)	48	1500 (1.5 litre)	6 cups

Note: The conversions above are approximate and have been rounded to the next figure for convenience and ease of use.